Fake Work

Fake Work

How I Began to Suspect Capitalism Is a Joke

Leigh Claire La Berge

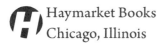
Haymarket Books
Chicago, Illinois

© 2025 Leigh Claire La Berge

Published in 2025 by
Haymarket Books
P.O. Box 180165
Chicago, IL 60618
www.haymarketbooks.org

ISBN: 979-8-88890-367-4

Distributed to the trade in the US through Consortium Book Sales and Distribution (www.cbsd.com) and internationally through Ingram Publisher Services International (www.ingramcontent.com).

This book was published with the generous support of Lannan Foundation, Wallace Action Fund, and Marguerite Casey Foundation.

Special discounts are available for bulk purchases by organizations and institutions. Please email info@haymarketbooks.org for more information.

Cover design by Michel Vrana.

Library of Congress Cataloging-in-Publication data is available.

10 9 8 7 6 5 4 3 2 1

Contents

Prologue: The Almost End of the World   vii

Phase I: Taking Inventory   1
Millennial Transitions ~ Quality Assurance ~ "Il n'y a pas de hors-texte" ~ Write What You Know ~ Teamwork

Phase II: Media and Mediations   75
My Putative Promotion ~ A Total Bitch and an Absolute Fraud ~ A Tepid Marxist and a Bubble Popped ~ My Joke of a Promotion

Phase III: Contingency Planning   143
Continental Comportment ~ Frequent Fliers ~ Floods and Fires ~ The End of the End

Afterward: Weeks and Decades   203

Acknowledgements   209
Notes   211

Prologue

The Almost End of the World

It is the case with most catastrophes that their sudden and unexpected appearance contributes a not inconsiderable part of their catastrophic form. Earthquakes. Wars. Pandemics. One moment's tranquility seems an impossible relation to the next one's chaos. As thankfully rare as such events are, perhaps it's rarer still to be given advance warning of the moment a world-historical calamity will strike. But denizens of the last millennium, those liming around the mid- to late 1990s—for whom laptop computers were not yet a necessity, for whom cell phones had a genuinely novel ring, and for whom the word "texting" would have likely had literary associations—they received this sort of prognostication early and often. They, we, actually, for I was one of them, were given heed that an event most unsettling, one whose scale would span the local and global, the individual and collective, might visit on December 31, 1999, at 11:59 p.m. and 59 seconds, and when it did, it could beset us all.

Its given name sounded robotic, with inflections both futuristic and antiquated. Y2K. As odd as those coordinates may seem, they did have their own precision. Y = year; 2 = the Arabic numeral 2; K = thousand, a nod to the Greek language in which *K* stands for *kilo*, analogous to "thousand." Taken together, Y2K declared in no uncertain terms: Year 2000. What about that date? Well, it might not arrive, and if it did, it might so transform our present that the world we knew before would be unrecognizable. ATMs wouldn't function. Planes wouldn't fly. Hour and minute hands on wristwatches would rotate counterclockwise. Year 2000. People had been anticipating this numerical milestone forever, but now, we were told, we'd be lucky if we survived it.

Technological in nature, Y2K would affect computers first, transforming them from machines of skill, putative cognition, and connectivity into lifeless heaps of metal, plastic, and glass. Soon thereafter, daily necessities and conveniences that our modern age had seen fit to computerize—oh, say, banks, supply chains, the New York City subway—would sputter and stall. Once computer technology had been felled, who could say what regressive social forces would emerge putsch-like into the newly created vacuum of social order: right-wing nut jobs, retired members of the Fraternal Order of Police, loons and goons of every imaginable stripe. "New York, Chicago, Atlanta, and a dozen other cities are going to resemble Beirut in January 2000.... The government of the U.S. as we currently know it will fail on 1/1/2000," conjectured one historical onlooker.[1]

Or not.

In fact, the third millennium arrived as seamlessly as the previous two had, even more so, if the historical record is to be believed. Messiahs weren't immaculately birthed, nor were continental crusades launched. And by the end of the first week of January of the long-awaited Year 2000, the once-prevailing idea that it all might have been for naught seemed as naive as that of putting away one's winter coat when a bucktoothed rodent failed to see its shadow on Groundhog Day. Prediction has never achieved the status of a science, of course, and divining the future is a habit better suited to Sophoclean tragedy than to hedging actual arcs of human history. Still, a quarter of a century later, today, in 2025, it seems reasonable and maybe even necessary to wonder: Have so many oracles ever gotten so much so wrong as those in the 1990s did? Has an expectation ever been met with the bathos of Y2K? Has an anticlimax ever been so deserving of its prefix?

Unless a world-turning event did occur in those early days of the third millennium, just not the one that was forecasted. It's a truism of psychoanalysis that the wrong idea might unwittingly introduce the right one. Instead of saying "I feel disappointed," a patient complains, "This therapy isn't working." That slight gives the analyst an opening. "Is there something else that isn't working?" she might inquire. "Well, now that you mention it . . . ," the patient follows.

Because things did go wrong in the third millennium, and they did so almost immediately. For one, the economy, the same one that was supposed to be new, different, unstoppable, the first of the great financial bubbles that define our day, the dot-com economy, turned in 2000 and fully soured by 2002. It was done in not by technological infelicity but by a group of fraudsters, yet it crashed nonetheless, and when it did, billions in value was erased, a recession was ushered in, and a chorus of "never agains" could be heard on Wall Street. The 2001 toppling of the World

Trade Center transpired alongside that burst economic bubble. A surprise, yes, but also in its own way another prediction gone awry. This one that geopolitical political crises were over; that history, in the sense of rupture, had ended with the collapse of the Soviet Union; and that, from 1991 on, everything on the world stage would be mostly fine. Instead, we've had twenty-plus years of global war. The economic collapse was an inside job. The World Trade Center collapse, the result of a foreign intrusion. Together they marked a termination of the Pax Americana of the 1990s, and jointly they instructed third-millennial Americans that our days would be peaceful and prosperous no more.

It's only fair that I include myself here, too. Like soothsayers of millennial transition, dot-com economy boosters, and post–Cold War foreign policy analysts, I misjudged the future and my place in it. And, in 1998, when I peered over the rumpled edges of my college graduation program—it was printed on both sides in a precocious nod to environmental conservation—daring to train my vision not on the alphabetized names of my newly BA-minted classmates but on the expanse of adult-tinted time and space that lay ahead of me, I likewise had a vision of uncertain grandiosity: I will be a businessman. The sort who makes money and wears suits. I'll read the *Wall Street Journal* and commute to Midtown Manhattan, I imagined. I'll attend weekly status meetings with corporate éminences grises named Guy. Certain items on the business trips I would take I planned to expense; others I would absorb the cost of myself. Enroll me in the employee stock plan and let the dividends accrue.

I'm quite sure I never plotted such a counterintuitive course for myself. But the nature of its genesis mattered not. It worked, and so did I. I was hired to work, that is, on a Y2K project, of all things, for a sprawling global conglomerate over whose imperial territory the sun never set. Or rather, I signed on to an anti-Y2K project, a kind of techno-prophylactic. If the end of modern technology did come on 12/31/1999, it wouldn't come for the Fortune 500 firm that employed me and placed me in its burgeoning millennial-preparedness office. I bought a suit that I indeed sometimes wore. I read the *Wall Street Journal* on my commute to Midtown. Status meetings were on Wednesdays. That my plan succeeded for a hot second is likely deserving of its own sociological study about who advances professionally and how, but this book doesn't investigate the many variances of what sociologists of class mobility call *distinction*.

Instead, *Fake Work: How I Began to Suspect That Capitalism Is a Joke* recounts how in getting it wrong, I also got it right. Because I was interested in businessmen, just not in being one myself. (Or in having dinner with them. Or sex.) The architecture of corporations fascinated me and still does, but while being employed by one, I learned that I need not personally inhabit the buildings that housed them to explore the intricacies of their construction. In a stultifying working world, I became intrigued by corporate work itself. And it was there, in the most capitalized place I've ever been or likely ever will be, that I discovered political economy—only its faintest shadows, true, but those became my ley lines to ancient forms of knowledge, like Karl Marx's *Capital*, volume 1. This book retraces my journey, detours—and there were plenty—and distractions, from Midtown to Marx and a little beyond.

Fake Work is real in that the story recounted here really did happen. I was employed by a multinational advertising conglomerate from 1998 to 2000. It was filled with suited businessmen who, whatever their differences in personality and character, whichever professional sports franchises they lauded or loathed, shared the common goal of saving global advertising from what seemed for all the world to be an impending Y2K disaster. So important the preservation of advertising appeared to these professional advertisers that this conglomerate engaged outside management consultants, the best and the brightest, to ensure its third-millennium continuation. In exchange for millions of dollars, those consultants designed and implemented a process (it was actually called The Process) to ensure that come what may on January 1, 2000, television commercials would run, billboards would stand tall, and 25–30 percent of every newspaper page would feature not current events but opportunistic come-ons for products and services.

Said hired management consulting firm, it turned out, was a fraud. But Y2K, it turned out, was also somewhat fraudulent. The world made modern by computer technology might have collapsed when the clock struck midnight—seriously? Was the world's technological infrastructure being driven by Cinderella's coach? Nor has advertising ever held a place in the pantheon of those industries considered essential to the flourishing of a democratic, compassionate, and educated society. Even the economy in which we were daily immersed in the late 1990s wasn't entirely legitimate. *Fake Work* recalls each of these aspects of what remains a surreal time in American economic history, and in my personal history, too. One could say that *Fake Work* is a real story about a fake one, and it's a tale I've wanted to relate for some time.

Because even as I toiled in corporate Midtown in the late 1990s, I had a sense that something was amiss. Not everything, which would have been more accurate, but a few things. That's why I began keeping notes, a business journal of sorts. Write enough and you've got a book, I soon learned. That book, my first and worst, the one I accidentally wrote in a Midtown skyscraper in the late 1990s, was never published—a fact for which I am thankful. But this book, the one in the here and now, *Fake Work*, is based on that one and uses bits and pieces of it as documentary evidence of the white-collar life I once led. Few would believe that during the corporate yarn I'm about to unfurl, I regularly flew to far-flung locales, like Santiago de Chile, for twenty-minute lunch meetings. I'm glad I still have the itineraries. Many would be surprised to learn that Fortune 500 status meetings don't have the academic rigor of a Cub Scout bake sale. I possess agendas.

More than evidence, though, in that original manuscript, I collected experience, namely that of seeing the global economy splayed out across the planet as a formaldehyde-doused rat might be on a high school lab table, stomach exposed, extremities pinned, ready for dissection. It was never my intent to wield a scalpel. I don't even eat meat! But let us say my hand was forced by the situation, one in which capitalism's most feted concepts— efficiency, merit, work itself—seemed, at their best, punchlines to good jokes. But they weren't usually at their best.

All of it would be easy enough to damn or dismiss, but that only gets a critic, in this case, me, so far. In such a sorry scene of lost time, environmental indifference, frittered-away resources, sexism, racism, homophobia, who, ultimately, is the joke on? Was I impressed into capital's service, stranded on the ship deck of one of its commercial fleet to the point where absconding would have left me marooned in a foreign port? Was I confined, calorie-less and exit-less, on a muddy feudal manor and forced to till soil for my daily rations? Hardly.

I wanted to work for this advertising conglomerate. And then I did. And while I had been advertised to my entire life, I had never considered advertisers people with whom I shared a polis, protagonists with hopes and dreams, fantasies and fears. If anything, advertising had assumed for me gnat-like characteristics. I found it annoying and irksome, more apparent in certain seasons and never more than skin-deep. What are advertisers like? I can report that they delight in puns. When one colleague whose last name doubled as a popular consumer goods producer—let's say it was Ford—had a child, my office reveled in noting that "a new model of Ford" had been released, that one could now "test drive a new Ford." Their profession produces brand loyalty, and they exhibit it themselves in quite genuine fashion. Run out of deodorant on a business trip? They won't slap on whatever's on offer at the hotel commissary. And substitute cigarettes? Forget it. They will sooner have the office receptionist FedEx a pack of their preferred smoke from New York City to Tokyo than take a drag on a stand-in brand.

I worked in a building of advertisers. We passed in the halls. We shared company lunches, usually ordered-in Japanese, offering, as it does, something for so many dietary preferences. But I worked with management consultants, perhaps best characterized as the organic intellectuals of the contemporary corporate scene. They don't do business; rather, they contemplate it. They "emerge from a specific social class and function to elaborate that class's productive activity as a set of general principles"; they undertake a "critical elaboration" of economic activities into a "new and integral conception of the world."[2] The best economic knowledge appears as unspecific, management consultants insist; abstract thought delivers more to the bottom line than discrete details do; any example may be interpreted through a larger concept, and they devise the concepts. They like to "leverage," to "problem solve," and to "innovate." They are "streamliners" and "consolidators." They might be said to deliberate in corporate philosophy, to be corporate philosophers themselves, even.

Which was certainly one of my points of entrée into the whole thing to begin with. In 1998, I was a philosopher, a certified one, if my undergraduate diploma counts, and management consulting seemed to me a philosophical enterprise. God knows it had more to recommend it than the debates then roiling American philosophy—Does a deracinated but functioning human brain floating in a vat of saline solution have consciousness? What is it like to be a bat?—and I had more pressing questions to contend with. Like, what kind of good life can one lead as a twenty-two-year-old unemployed philosopher? As I had absorbed narratives of the 1990s dot-com economy with the directness of a nicotine patch, I, too, had onboarded a favorite incantation of liberal arts' marketing departments. "What can you do with a liberal arts degree?" its skeptics ask. "Anything!" its boosters answer. In a way that's true. I did do a lot during my corporate tour, and it changed me.

I now appreciate a good ad campaign.

I still drink Diet Pepsi.

I continue to subscribe to the *Wall Street Journal*.

But in another way, I couldn't do what I wanted to, which was to understand the workings of late second-millennial capitalism. One can't do that with a liberal arts degree, at least I couldn't. It remains an open question whether the fault lay with me or with my teachers. My mission was complicated by the fact that I didn't know that's what I wanted to do. But then again, a liberal arts education might have helped me locate and refine the language of my ambition. Instead, I was spoon-fed a liquid diet of poststructuralism and classical political theory, Kool-Aid I metabolized on my way to corporate America.

Time was short and the end was looming. It's almost as if my corporate life happened in dog years. Within eight months of my hiring, I had assumed a managerial position—true, a fake one, but working with a fraudulent management consultancy on a fictitious problem, that hardly distinguished it. Within a year, I had become a seasoned global business traveler, one as comfortable on the steamy sidewalks of Hong Kong as on the baroque boulevards of Buenos Aires, a regular at London's Heathrow Airport Admirals Lounge and indeed something of a rear admiral myself. Meeting with senior advertising colleagues the world over, I asked them directly and usually sincerely, If modern technology vanished in a Y2K meltdown, what would their advertising operations look like? Within a year and a half, it was all over. My position, not the world.

I caught the tail end of an economic bubble, and I'm glad that I did. The funny thing was then and remains now that my experience of the best corporate America had to offer was still somewhat off-putting, and, given every inducement to stay, I elected to quit working as a businessman and to begin writing about economic history—the vantage point from which I today return to this episode. So maybe I did behold exactly what I desired, a front-row seat to one of the more absurd economic spectacles ever mounted: capitalism attempting to save the world from its imaginary, self-inflicted, and seemingly certain destruction, bringing me along for the ride and asking me to take notes.

A note on the documentation: Some of the names and identifying details of people and companies mentioned in this book have been changed. Arthur Andersen LLP has been legally defunct since 2002. "The Conglomerate" refers to a large, extant communications holding company where I worked.

Phase I:
Taking Inventory

Millennial Transitions

My first professional and only corporate position was fake. From 1998 to 2000, I worked as an analyst with a team of consultants and auditors from Arthur Andersen LLP, shortly before that lauded firm's fraudulent activities were revealed, it surrendered its accounting license, and was shuttered. I did not work *for* Arthur Andersen. Such a blue-chip firm would never have hired the likes of me. They recruited from places like Harvard. I graduated from Hampshire College. They required new hires to have impeccable GPAs. My college didn't confer grades. But more than any of the necessary entries on a potential employee's resume—most of which I lacked—I didn't possess the sympathy and orientation to develop such skills. The absences that marked my professional history were related to decisions I had made in adolescence, possibly earlier. No one event had determined my career trajectory; rather, a cumulative selection shaped its path. Like abandoning extracurricular activities for the Grateful Dead circa 1992 or the time I included a poorly sketched Tyrannosaurus rex in my local flora and fauna journal for AP Bio. By the time I realized how much I was missing, incidentally the same time I needed a professional position, wanted one, longingly, even, it was too late to catch up.

Nonetheless, in certain rare moments within the history of capitalism, too few workers exist. Not as an absolute, of course;

in total, workers always outnumber paid possibilities for work. That's how our economy functions. But in a specific industry a shortage may emerge, if only for a brief time. During these economic exceptions, those who are sought after often attribute their desirability to their own aptitude or accomplishments. I never did. And on my first day of work *with* Arthur Andersen LLP, it was clear that some aberration in accumulation had placed me in a twenty-fourth-floor Midtown Manhattan conference room overlooking the Museum of Modern Art's sculpture garden, sitting amidst curiously run-down office furniture and staring at a PowerPoint slide of a cartoon duck, bespectacled and yellow, presented from side profile, holding a sledgehammer over its beaked head and preparing to smash a desktop computer.

It was a fake job because although I worked with Arthur Andersen, they never hired me. Rather, I worked for a global advertising conglomerate who had hired Andersen on a consultancy project and then placed me alongside the Andersen team—the result of a confluence of staffing shortages. And it was a fake job because Andersen was faking it; the firm spent the late 1990s certifying fraudulent financial statements from Enron, the Texas-based energy company that made "financial derivatives" a household phrase, until that company went bankrupt in a cloud of scandal and suicide and Andersen was convicted of obstruction of justice for destroying its Enron-related documents. And, finally, it was a fake job because the problem that this conglomerate had hired Andersen to solve was not real, at least not real in the sense of needing to be solved or of them being able to solve it.

That problem was Y2K, sometimes known as the Year 2000, or as the Y2K bug, and it prophesied that on January 1, 2000, computers' internal clocks would be unable to process the change in thousands digit and hundreds digit as 1999 became 2000, would crash, and would take with them whatever technology they were operating, from email to television to air traffic control to, really, the technological infrastructure of global modernity. Hospitals might have emergency power generators to stave off the worst effects (unless the generators, too, succumbed to the Y2K bug), but not so advertising firms. One agency after another could go offline, setting off a chain of failed commercials and who knew what else. For a global advertising conglomerate, such a scenario would be a business disaster. And that's what the duck was about. Or at least functioned as some kind of allegory for. Because ducks hate technology? Or have some unique knowledge of computing? I couldn't be sure. But as this was a presentation for new employees, I thought it better not to ask.

My new position was the type I had for months aspired to—coveted, in fact. From employment agency to employment agency I had traipsed, through a Manhattan August so soggy one could grasp the humidity like a handful of wet sand, only to be told in a manner that ranged from gently dismissive to hurriedly curt that the positions I sought required "top schools and top scores." I had neither, and the most creative rendering of the odd chronological collection of personal facts that passed for my résumé wouldn't amend the problem. What I needed was a deus ex machina.

Reader, I found one. Or, rather, one found me: Y2K.

With a world-ending scenario on the horizon, standards, it seemed, were being relaxed. Economic historians contend that "the golden age of American capitalism" occurred between 1945 and 1973. As its European competitors smoldered in a postwar rubble, as labor unions got in line and got paid, as the federal government underwrote universities and industries alike, the American system worked with a pace and plentitude it never had before, nor has since. I'd date those halcyon days of bounty a bit later, at the personal level at least, from 1998 to 2000, during the dot-com bubble when capital's gilt still shone, if examined from certain discrete angles and with propitious lighting.

I intercepted capitalism at a serendipitous, if puzzling, moment, one of strange confluence whereby legions of corporate and legal actors thought that a technological rupture powerful enough to wreak gale-force infrastructural havoc might descend when the clock struck midnight on the last December evening of 1999 and ordered that teams be put in place to ensure social and economic continuity and selected me for one of them. An understanding of that unlikely intersection demands genealogies both autobiographical and historical that follow me and Y2K. They travel parallel paths and become coterminous sometime in the otherwise inauspicious year of 1998.

Indeed, in a manner likely similar to those mid-twentieth-century programmers who rendered the first two digits of many computers' four-digit year slot immutable at "19" and who no doubt thought that the need to represent a year 2000 in computers' internal calendars was far enough off that either their code would be amended or it would be irrelevant by that date's arrival, I had not considered a professional career among life's possibilities. I thought, as they surely did, that something else will happen. More than that fantasy of someone else cleaning up our problems, Y2K and I shared a certain historical isomorphism—yet we had missed each other for decades despite multiple opportunities for casual introduction. Both the event and I were born in that often overlooked but economically crucial decade of the 1970s. As a toddler, I had little economic volition aside from an amateur collector's obsession with those specially minted bicentennial quarters. But my parents had to suffer through the Carter recession, and they did so unaware that the society slowly computerizing around them was laying within it the seeds of its own undoing.

Both Y2K and I had a careless youth during the inflated and inflationary 1980s. There I was, happy as a clam, playing *Pac-Man* and *Frogger* at the local Pizza Hut. If someone had told me that the very consoles that hosted my video games contained within them a computerized calendar, that the calendar might malfunction, and that video games might go extinct in 1999, I am sure I would have felt a shiver of concern. But no one did.

The subterranean problems that attended each of us were unearthed in the Clintonian 1990s, when it became clear that some instance of foresight had gone awry. In the case of Y2K, a once-small problem of calendrical computation had been replicated and distributed into a larger system, and now no one could predict where or how it would reverberate. Throughout the early 1990s, magazines like *PC Weekly* had offered occasional warnings and had broadcast their own anxious moments, as had speakers at evangelical churches and participants on electronic bulletin boards, that 1990s iteration of social media. This could be the big one, *Computerworld* intimated, humanity's Frankenstein moment when technology begins giving marching orders to those who created it:

> Have you ever been in a car accident? Time seems to slow down as you realize you're going to crash into the

car ahead of you. It's too late to avoid it—you're going to crash. All you can do now is watch it happen. The information systems community is heading toward an event more devastating than a car crash. We are heading toward the year 2000.[1]

In the case of me, a larger problem—Why do people need to work? What a terrible way to organize an individual existence, to say nothing of a society—had lodged itself squarely in my own life. I had to contend with the rather urgent need to join the ranks of those with full-time employment.

There's a final bit of temporal coincidence that is perhaps the most important one. Both Y2K and my early twenties now dwell firmly in the past. Y2K has been forgotten, and likely for good reason. Nothing happened, after all, and now it seems like a misbegotten, poorly conceived historical drama, akin, perhaps, to Orson Welles's 1938 radio broadcast of *The War of the Worlds* when some portion of the audience missed that it was a radio *play* and thought bellicose Martians had touched down in New Jersey. My early twenties, too, seem long gone and full of questionable judgment, but they remain accessible to me. And unlike Y2K, the mark of the transition lingers, not only the millennial one from 1999 to 2000 but the one from parental ward to independent actor, from adolescent to adult, from college to career.

I still have anxiety dreams about the possible missing forms, incomplete requirements, and improperly signed documents that occasioned the changeover. They aren't really about the paperwork, of course. Rather, they are concerned with what I did and didn't do to prepare for adulthood, a sort of liberal arts hangover, a feeling—even now—that I overlooked a crucial part of being educated. Some of this nervous hesitation I attribute to my collegiate advisor, a physiologically and characterologically sharp second-wave feminist philosopher whose understandable bitterness about academia resulted in her attempting to sway students to her own cause célèbre: that she was treated poorly by her colleagues, one in particular. In place of textual exegesis or checking the completion of a proof, she often reflected on one of ancient philosophy's areas of inquiry, the good life, which, she explained, had been foreclosed. Such personalized pedagogy is why parents pay top dollar for the small classes and self-designed majors of an alternative liberal arts school, and our relationship did direct me away from philosophy, likely for the better.

It also compromised whatever emotional reserves I might have summoned for my launch out of middle-class American teenage-hood, of which college is the final bookend, and before my health insurance went the way of my dining hall meal card, I sought counsel for my nervous ailments. So obviously symptomatic was I that my presentation wouldn't have been out of place in Freud's fin de siècle hysteria investigations. But alas, the precipice on which I stood hovered over a different century's end, and my visit to the campus health clinic offered a refillable sedative prescription in place of enlightenment or even basic inquiry. Anything going on that might be causing stress? someone, anyone, might have wondered. I probably would have said no and done so genuinely; as it were, the only therapists I would see that first, postgraduate summer were "job placement counselors," as commission-seeking agents at NYC employment offices had begun to refer to themselves. My Klonopin June included weeks of a slightly disorienting, if relaxing, daze, but I would be inaccurately describing that drug's efficacy if I attributed to it my first major postgraduate decision. I planned to move to New York and join the ranks of management consulting.

Try though I have, I can't quite retrace the precise sequence of judgments that led to this somewhat phantasmatic commitment. There lurked a class fantasy, certainly. My own experience of tennis camp while in middle school—an elite sleepaway deal about which my mother accurately predicted, "You'll be the poorest person there"—no doubt played a role. Who were these people and their parents? Before tennis camp, they had done a stint at sailing or golf camp; they were standing members of NELTA, the New England Lawn Tennis Association, while I'd been mowing actual lawns for four bucks an hour under the southern sun.

Beyond the imprecations of my moody advisor, college, too, had left a certain impression. Not the college I attended but the prestigious neighboring institutions at which I took history of philosophy classes, Smith and Amherst. Their graduates were destined for further prestigious institutions—banks, consulting firms, professional schools—in what I was now starting to apprehend was a pattern that didn't augur terribly well for me. Elite standing confers elite standing. Add to that a stubborn character flaw, one that some future iteration of the *Diagnostic and Statistical Manual of Mental Disorders* might include as a strand of oppositional personality disorder. I have a tendency to develop a curiosity about things that I dislike, one which invariably places me in dislikable environments, even as it does offer ample chances to catalogue my frustrations.

All of life's little narrative threads and unanalyzed idiosyncrasies had somehow sedimented in a desire to answer a question whose very articulation assumed only the faintest of specifics:

What was it like to be a businessman? Why did they get paid so handsomely? Their sense of entitlement, what was it to, exactly? Same for the pace with which they traversed Grand Central Station: Where were they going and what was their hurry? Even their briefcases I found rather captivating. Their slim dimensions revealed that they didn't hold much content-wise, but they were clutched and carried with such dedication that it seemed unlikely that they were mere accoutrement to a corporate working day.

One interest I didn't have, a kind of farcical omission, in retrospect, is the one that now seems most crucial. What is business? I'd never cared for it, and as for Adam Smith's claim that it's human nature to "truck, barter and exchange," I could only wonder if I fell outside the curve. Management consulting, then, seemed the sensible choice. It offered something for those who were disinclined to manage but appealed to those who might consult about management. In this construction, I saw a connection to my own training: philosophy does not solve problems, it consults about them, and even then, most philosophers do not attend to actual problems; rather, they focus on ones they themselves conjure, with no topic too pointless or anti-intuitive. In fact, my familiarity with imaginary problems offered an unexpected boon to my Y2K-focused corporate rotation. Moreover, management consulting afforded what I imagined the right coordinates of adulthood to be: a weekday destination between 9:00 a.m. and 5:00 p.m.-ish, a salary, and other sundries I couldn't enumerate but was sure existed.

You can imagine my disappointment, then—it seemed almost a form of private persecution—when I learned from the headhunting firms that I had begun to visit that twenty-two-year-olds don't actually get hired at management consultancies. McKinsey & Company; Booz Allen Hamilton; Arthur Andersen LLP, these outfits don't allow walk-ins as a discount hair salon might. Instead, such firms recruit. From colleges. Only they didn't recruit at alma maters like mine, a school where, before the regional accreditation body visited, a few students had graffitied scare quotes around the hilltop sign so that it read Hampshire "College" as it welcomed the accreditors. Not only that, instead of being sought out and convinced, instead of being wanted and wooed, the job counselors seemed to have a rather inverted understanding of any potential liaison we might share. I would need to prove myself *to them*. And knowledge of less-examined sinews in the history of political philosophy, my only real skill, if you could call it that, was not given much consideration.

Rather, like a military enlistee destined for an undecided training regime, my job search included a battery of timed technical tests. Word, Excel, PowerPoint, facility with these members of the Microsoft Office Suite became markers of achievement, as did my typing ability. The subtle message such trials offered was one of competition: some PowerPoint users, those who could easily embed a video into a slide, for example, would fare better than others. Any meaning to be gleaned from the content of the typing test I took had a more declarative presentation:

```
The business environment has
undergone a dramatic change in the
last half a century. Fifty years
ago, an employee could expect to
find a job right after high school
or college and work there until
```

```
he or she retired. In today's
highly competitive marketplace
however, job security is virtually
impossible to find. Managers are
laid off without a warning, and many
employees fall prey to downsizing,
a lot of workers are forced to take
early retirement before they are
ready. In today's highly unstable
job market, workers must realize
the absence of job security and
take responsibility for their
career development.
```

As my fingers replicated the paragraph, my mind remained suspended between the moral lesson on offer and the need for digital agility; all keystrokes were monitored, from backspaces to hard returns to swipes at the space bar. One too many or too few might derail me. I clocked in at fifty-three words a minute, with six recognized mistakes. The job counselor who communicated to me the results of my aptitude tests said they were inconclusive, as though I had sat for a medical panel, but had I, further tests would have been ordered. Instead, I entered this agency's rotation—they'd call me.

This wasn't the New Economy of the late '90s I had been told to expect. The one that was everywhere, an agent of change, the one I was led to believe was embracing youth, diversity, even a certain amount of antiauthoritarianism. As well, a tight labor market in knowledge workers had emerged as one millennium prepared to welcome the next and as a new breed of firm, based on the internet and called "dot-coms" after the grammar of URLs, was angling to dominate the emergent world of e-commerce. Flush with cash, these internet companies were hoovering up any possessors of knowledge they could find. If you could place an *e* in front of a noun and deploy a hyphen, you could wrangle a few million dollars of venture capital funding and start a dot-com—e-desserts, e-knickknacks, e-skateboards, e-calendar—and once you did, you needed employees. Friends from my grade-less college whose only experience in business had been parking lot drug deals were now talking stock options. I, meanwhile, had been offered a position selling portable water filters on commission after responding to a vague classified in the back pages of the *Times*.

Were it not for the need to feed, clothe, and house myself, I likely would have given up. Alas, the requirements of basic subsistence have a way of keeping one going. The agency that finally conducted me to full employment, Careers by Penthouse, required no tests, asked few questions, and seemed to allow its employees to smoke. Its naff 1970s aesthetic of maroon velour curtains and faux wood-paneled walls recalled more the pornographic magazine than it did a coveted top floor. I appreciated its compromised and unprofessional appearance at once. Even its location distinguished it. Far from the white-collar avenues of Manhattan's tony East Side, the place abutted the Port Authority bus terminal—one got a dusting of Greyhound exhaust on every entrance and departure.

Unlike other employment agencies, concerned as they were with metrics and results, this one made no categorical distinction between knowing something and knowing about it. JavaScript, for example, a computer programming language, was one that I knew about but did not know. Fine. And the identity of the firm, the one that the chest-hair-exposing job counselor hinted might actually employ me? There I drew a total epistemological blank. "Oh really?" he said without a trace of scorn but with some genuine bafflement. "It's only one of the biggest goddamned communications companies in the world." And then the dramatic one, the world-ender. The position available was Y2K-specific, and the job counselor needed to know whether I was aware that the modern technology might go on a catastrophic hiatus of unknown duration at the end of 1999. In fact, I had heard of something to that effect, although if pressed—thankfully I wasn't—I couldn't have explicated. Nor did the scene of an ensuing apocalypse concern me. If I had to assume a millenarian posture to get hired, so be it. Conversely, if the role required something of stoicism in the face of techno-eschatology, I felt confident I could present that affect, too. Like a biblical flood, I would rise to the occasion.

Quality Assurance

If there's a Proustian madeleine of my Fortune 500 life that continues to pull me into the past, that evokes a corporate nostalgia and longing, neither of which qualifies as enjoyable but both of which are uncannily mesmerizing, it's calling an 800 number. Not the opening instruction to take care in making one's selection because "some menu options have changed." Haven't they always? No, it's the just-as-dependable mention of surveillance and information collection, the oddly menacing warning that "this call may be recorded for quality assurance." Who adjudicates the quality of those phone calls, parsing the transcript for inconsistencies in meaning and intent? Who keeps the call records, and where are they stored? Before I walked into this advertising conglomerate's Y2K outpost for my Careers by Penthouse–arranged job interview, I can honestly say I had more interest in contemplating the filament of a toothpaste tube than in considering such questions. But it was quality assurance that gave me my in and offered me not only a job but a career with my business desideratum—management consulting.

A potentially world-ending technological implosion. One of the biggest goddamned communications companies in the world. A looming, glassy Midtown skyscraper. I imagined the blinking color palate of NASA's Mission Control or the rapid transiting of letters and numbers across the New York Stock Exchange's trading floor, not the 8.5-by-11-inch single sheet sign that was taped to the seemingly indifferent door. Conglomerate2000, the office was called, a simple enough name. This outpost would deal with the predicted and actual ramifications of the Year 2000 bug for the Conglomerate, itself a holding company of more than 1,100 communications firms ranging from advertising, to branding, to marketing, to public relations.

In fact, during my initial interview at the Conglomerate, no specific mention of doomsday occurred. Nor of advertising. Or management consulting. There was no discussion, even, of the rainy weather, and few pleasantries were exchanged. Rather, I spent about twelve minutes with a laconic, mustachioed, middle-aged Arthur Andersen manager named Guy. On his otherwise empty desk sat a colorful carved wooden figure of a boy wearing overalls and dangling his feet over a quaint pier in a recognizable fishing posture. Yet he held a golf club. "Gone Golfing," the plinth's etched letters declared. "On a scale of one to ten, what's your knowledge of computer software?" Guy began. I paused for a moment, unsure of whether our interview would include a demonstrative component, as had my visits to so many employment agencies. But his office was empty, save his laptop, strangely locked to the arm of his swivel chair with one of those plastic-sheathed steel cords, and his golfing tchotchke. I couldn't see how he would test me. I said "eight" and we moved on.

Guy was my second stop during the Conglomerate interview. The first had been with the Managing Director, who, in a scene that may read as contrived for its stereotypical polarity, glanced at my resume and asked with a perplexed mien, "You worked at the ACLU?" I had been a summer intern, the previous summer, the one before my Klonopin daze. I copyedited the *Reproductive Rights* newsletter and answered the phone during the receptionist's lunch break. If asked, I would have reported that the ACLU's main switchboard functions as a kind of national clearinghouse for those with undiagnosed psychotic tendencies. But I wasn't. "Well, I think they're basically a good organization that takes a lot of shit," the director concluded before conveying me to Guy and explaining as he did so that the Conglomerate2000 office had two corporate populations, those who worked for Arthur Andersen on the Conglomerate's Y2K project and those who worked for the Conglomerate itself. If hired, I'd be a kind of dual passport holder. I'd work *for* one, but *with* the other. And it was that other with whom I now sat.

"And what's your knowledge of computer hardware, on a scale of one to ten?" Guy continued. The moment called for both boldness and modesty. I felt committed to "eight," a number I had long appreciated for its intimations of infinity when turned sideways. So I repeated myself, "Eight." Here I should add that one of my campus work-study jobs had been as a computer lab monitor. I could restart a PC or refill a printer's paper tray if the situation demanded it, although it rarely did as I had the weekend evening shifts.

And then came his penultimate question, the one that would determine the development of my nascent career. Given the exacting reputation of Arthur Andersen and the potentially apocalyptic setting of our encounter, one might expect the summa of Guy's inquiry to be grand and revelatory, biblical even: What animals would populate your diluvian arc? Maybe survivalist: With which provisions would you stock your earthen bunker? Something technical would surely have been appropriate: Which programming language is most vulnerable, which most impregnable? But inscrutable Guy stayed the course, a characteristic that I would learn indeed defined him. "And what's your level of problem-solving, on a scale of one to ten?" he asked. There would be no SAT scores—mine had been decidedly average, but the whole test had been redesigned and its scores recalibrated soon after I took it, and now few people could make sense of the older results; no college transcripts; no career office to steer certain students to certain institutions; no typing tests or PowerPoint competitions. My twenty-two-years' worth of infelicities—some given to me, more cultivated by me—suddenly seemed surmountable.

Indeed, I suspected then, in August 1998, and can confirm now, that a working life presents few loopholes, an economic term whose genealogy has relevance here. Originally a cleave in a wall, an actual hole out of which to shoot an arrow, its meaning metamorphized into the process by which a business gets away with something designed, but not well designed, not to be gotten away with. Since that initial semantic shift, so many businesses have gotten away with so many things that the definition has transformed again to include giving a business a chance to get away with something with the hope that only a few entities will utilize it. The point is that as my professional and educational history, my aptitude, my credentials, my person, even, as each of these were recombined and transmuted into something called "problem-solving," only to be then reduced to an undefined scale of 1–10, I sensed an opportunity to pass through a corporate loophole. "Nine," I replied.

"That was it?" My girlfriend chirped when I reported to her the pinnacle of my day's transactions.

Guy had approved me, and the Conglomerate hired me on the spot. How could something not be off, and fundamentally so? Neither one of us had an answer, nor was I myself too inclined to investigate further. The infrastructure on offer appeared respectable enough. A Fortune 500 entity with all the trappings. The company was listed on the New York Stock Exchange and issued quarterly reports. There were suited men. And daily hauls of the *Wall Street Journal*, the *Financial Times*, the *New York Times*, plus a new one, *Adweek*, placed around the ground-floor lobby if seemingly never disturbed. But most crucially, the Conglomerate acted in one way exceptional. They took me. Dayenu—said girlfriend was Jewish—had they only hired me, it would have been enough. But there was more. In a career twist whose origins remain murky, I was placed on the Quality Assurance Team, work carried out exclusively by the Arthur Andersen contingent.

They weren't called "a contingent" around the Y2K office, of course; rather, they were referred to as "the Andersen people," a term that indicated that a certain partition existed between them and other Conglomerate employees, from whom they commanded both bewilderment and respect and, as often follows from the first two, a certain amount of cynicism and resentment. Such contradictory feelings stemmed from the fact that management consultants constituted then, and still do now, the vanguard of corporate work. They transit between companies and industries, parachuting in to diagnose problems and suggest, although rarely implement, best practice solutions. That's management consulting lingo, *best practice*, and it indicates that the good is not enough—this isn't D. W. Winnicott's consulting room—rather, management consultants aim for superlatives.

They hire the best. They practice the best. They claim former mayor of South Bend, Indiana, former United States secretary of transportation, Pete Buttigieg, among their alumni ranks. At the Conglomerate, the twenty or so Andersen people had their own offices, their own meetings, their own schedules, all of which took place within the Conglomerate's twenty-fourth-floor office space while they were on its project, but when they "rolled off" (they had their own terminology, too), they would take up residence within the ambit of another Andersen client.

In a certain way, then, I had landed what I had hoped for, and in an elite management consulting company, both colloquially and structurally, there I stood, an Andersen team member—had I ever wanted something so discrete and eventful and actually gotten it? In another way, however (perhaps several of them), my facsimile appearance of inclusion served for numerous occasions of exclusion. "You've been selected because you're Andersen quality but not Andersen price," the Quality Assurance Team's leader, Cindy, a chipper data-warehousing expert, explained on my second full day of work, as though I were a piece of organic fruit found amongst the conventional produce bin. She then related in an officious but friendly manner that as with wolves, pack solidity was as intense within Andersen groupings as it was offensive of intruders.

In the first meeting with my lupine team, I did stand out, though not for lack of credentials. Rather, I was the only one not massaging a fistful of Play-Doh. The office in which we met was beige, the carpet beige, the people beige, too. But from each Quality Assurance Team member's hands exploded a most brilliant collection of colors: neon greens and yellows, hot pink, siren red, an almost psychedelic scene. Team members twirled and juggled their own handfuls, separated their mass and recombined it; the only thing more impressive than their dexterity was their nonchalance. "It's a new management technique," Cindy noted to me, as an aside, answering a question I didn't have the courage to ask but one she had the perspicacity to know I was worriedly pondering—why am I the only QA Team member without a canister of Play-Doh? As she shifted her own oblong shape between her hands, she explained, "It helps relieve stress and streamline your thoughts." The irony that the one truly in need went without seemed lost on everyone. Nor did Cindy herself seem stressed—maybe because of the Play-Doh—but the situation she laid out for our team was certainly overwhelming.

The Conglomerate's 1,100-plus advertising, public relations, and communications companies worldwide spanned emerging markets and well-established ones. Each kicked up a certain percentage of their take to corporate headquarters, cumulatively raking in billions of dollars a year. But any or all of these "shops," in industry lexicon, might collapse on January 1, 2000, thus preventing the Conglomerate from executing its contractually agreed-to global advertising operations, compromising its earnings, exposing it to lawsuits, and jeopardizing its stock price. Maybe a radio station in Finland goes haywire and can't run a Conglomerate-booked spot; maybe a billboard tumbles off a highway in Rio de Janeiro amidst social chaos, and with it falls a Conglomerate-created visual; conceivably, a television station in Western Australia could disappear and, along with it, a Conglomerate-produced commercial. If such events were to transpire, the scene would be one in which revenue loss would be an almost best-case scenario; one could imagine far worse. There had been a slide in the New Hire Presentation, the one with the duck, that narrated the possibilities through a sexless stick figure, whose face was composed of a series of hurried dashes, who had a thought bubble hovering above its perfectly circular head, and who wondered, "On January 1, 2000, will I still have electricity, food, telephone, transportation, . . . ?" Each life-sustaining noun was contained in its own thought bubble a tad above and to the right of the previous one, and the final thought bubble offered only a series of anxiety-producing question marks.

Reminders of that same tremulous atmosphere appeared around the office, whose windowless kitchenette offered several copies of the book *Time Bomb 2000* for employees to peruse while they warmed their instant coffee or selected a Pepsi product—Pepsi being a client—from the mini fridge; the office bulletin board hosted a thumbtacked photocopy of a *Computerworld* article entitled "Noted Economist Predicts Y2K Recession" to greet team members on their daily arrival and departure from the elevator bay. A certain part of me felt foolish, I admit. To think I had been conducting myself as though a long-term future could be assumed. I'd even signed up for a discounted gym membership that required a two-year commitment. At least I wasn't the only one with a questionable sense of historical duration. When completing my onboarding process at the Conglomerate's HR office a couple of blocks east of its Y2K office, I was told that after six months I could elect to purchase company stock at a special employee rate—now I realized such a short window didn't allow much time for it to accrue value.

That said, the urgency of our historical predicament contrasted with the pace of the working day I soon found myself structured by, like the difference between an elapse of a second compared to a change of seasons. But it felt slower. The Andersen people had offices, but I was not an Andersen person, and my ramshackle Formica cubicle sat directly left of the receptionist, whose radio's ongoing broadcast of 1010 WINS's "minute by the minute" reporting marked the passage of time in place of natural light or human contact. "Traffic on the nines," "Weather on the ones." In the morning, the repetition of these phrases enervated me, doomed as I was to hear them every ten minutes; by afternoon, they seemed more encouraging, sometimes able to jolt me from the fluorescent fugue I had invariably slipped into.

Just as any previous notion I had of the elite character of the management consulting labor in which I was supposedly engaged stood in some contrast to the proofreading of inventory spreadsheets that now structured my life. The first segment of the Conglomerate's Y2K project, "Phase I: Inventory," took its name from the fact that most team members' activities were devoted to either retrieving inventories from the Conglomerate's various 1,100-plus agencies and imputting the data from those inventories into a database or checking for errors team members had made while doing so. The lesser-educated network analysts completed the data entry; the Ivy League–graduated Andersen Quality Assurance Analysts (and I) provided the oversight as we identified and recorded the mistakes our colleagues had committed. Someone had hit the 0 instead of its keyboard neighbor, the 9; a team member who had never questioned her ability to mirror write had typed 91 when she had meant to type 19; another team member, her mind wandering perhaps, had neglected to check the "entry completed" box. History would not judge such oversights kindly. My team set out to rectify them before it had the chance. Not rectify as in fix; rather, our charge was to alert the necessary interlocutors to the problem so that they could make amendments.

It was the mission of the Quality Assurance Team to ensure the quality of the Inventory Database. The verb under whose sign we labored was a new one for me: "to q.a."; its past tense "q.a.'ed." All mistakes our q.a.-ing located were recorded; all records of our q.a-ing were photocopied; the copies were kept in Cindy's office, while the originals were bound for a secure document warehouse in New Jersey, one whose safeguards included humidity control and fireproofing and whose precise location was not shared with the lowest professional strata of our team, me, for example, out of proprietary concern for their well-being. Necessarily, our records would be kept in paper. If the predicted Doomsday 2000 did arrive, the digital world would be inaccessible, if not disappeared. Computer technology had gotten us into this millennial quagmire, and, therefore, it would not be trusted to extricate us from it. That's why my answer of "nine" to Guy's invitation to rate my problem-solving abilities on a scale of one to ten during my interview had likely been more appreciated than my answer of "eight" in response to his invitation to rate my knowledge of computer software and hardware on a scale, possibly the same one, possibly a different one, of one to ten. The fact that the scale itself remained undefined and that neither interviewer nor interviewee agreed to its coordinates suggested both the fake nature of the whole endeavor as well as the desperation the Conglomerate felt to staff its Y2K office with sixteen months to prepare for the possible expiration of the modern technology.

Also odd appeared the fact that in the face of an impending total or partial technological suspension, the Andersen-developed office mantra stated that "Y2K is a documentation problem, not a technology problem." That had been in the New Hire Presentation, too, drafted, I later learned, by Cindy and approved by Guy, senior onsite manager of the Andersen people and firm partner-in-waiting. The message was declared in capitalized bold and italicized letters and encapsulated in a text box, and it appeared twice, as an announcement at the beginning, as a reminder at the end. While the technical problems that loomed on our collective corporate horizon may have been able to be fixed, one couldn't know of their status on January 1, 2000, with complete certainty until that revelatory day arrived. In some philosophical traditions that distance between what one thinks will happen and what does happen is the very definition of *the future*, but in the Conglomerate's Y2K office, it was understood as a problem in need of a work-around.

With the precocity for which they were known in business quarters, the Andersen people had located one. Instead of fixing things with the hope that they would function *tomorrow*—one foot always in the uncertain future—we would document anti-Y2K efforts that the Conglomerate had already undertaken, one foot in the past, by no means transparent but perhaps more knowable than those events not yet in existence. Instead of promising things to come, we would certify that things that had already transpired had been appropriately recorded. To the somewhat alarming claim of the Y2K town criers—there is no assurance of modern life after 12/31/1999—the Quality Assurance Team operated in retrospect: whatever happened yesterday, we would represent and consign to a database. And at a certain point, all that had happened yesterday was our documenting, so then we documented that. Then, exponentially, we had to document ourselves documenting our own documentation.

Skeptics, and I include myself, will immediately conjecture: What does any of this have to do with the potential malfunction of a computer's calendars on a systemwide level? How does knowing what a given advertising agency has in its inventory forestall time bomb 2000? How does checking that said agency's inventory matches the information we had in our inventory database get any of us to the other side of 1/1/2000? How does our documenting of our own documentation further our mission of ensuring the continuation of advertising after the dawn of the third millennium? A singular answer to these questions exists, but to comprehend it with the dedication it deserves requires a philosopher's commitment to exegesis.

"Il n'y a pas de hors-texte"

"Is it French?" people often ask of my first name, Leigh, which is some Anglo combination of old English and Irish. They ask in part because of my middle name, Claire, which is of French origin, but also Irish. Claire by itself, however, would be unlikely to generate a request for explanation. The real intrigue likely comes from the fact that as a southerner I was saddled with a usage of both first and middle names, Leigh and Claire, and some significant portion of my life's interlocutors have, on introduction, misheard "Leigh" as the French definite article *le*, as in *le chat*, "the cat." "Leigh" and *le* don't sound similar, nor are they spelled similarly; *le* is in fact masculine, and were I to have an article attached to my name, it would the feminine, *la*. And here we encounter a final confusion, one stemming from the fact that my last name is also French and does have a definite article in it, a feminine one. "La Berge" means "the riverbank." By the time we've gotten this far, whomever I happen to have just met is all but guaranteed to ask whether I speak French or am French and when I say no to both questions, I often note a sense of disappointment.

So let me be clear (one of the meanings of "Claire"): I have lived in France and visited that Norman country regularly. My paternal grandfather immigrated to the United States from

Francophone Quebec and both my parents spoke French. *Objet d'art* and *vichyssoise* were terms as common as *movie* and *popcorn* on my family's .25-acre suburban homestead. I may not "know" French, but I do know about it. I can read some French, too. A philosopher must. And one of that language's phrases accompanied me through college and became a kind of cipher I took recourse to as I attempted to decode my new corporate surroundings in autumn 1998: "il n'y a pas de hors-texte" (there is nothing outside of the text). Reality follows the text; the text does not record reality. Reality might not even exist; it might itself just be a text. And that's where I sat daily in my new Fortune 500 life. In the text. In an inventory spreadsheet, to be exact. When I finished q.a.-ing one of them, there was another to take its place, and then another after that. When I peered over the shoddy Formica partition of my cubicle, I saw other QA Team members, Andersen ones, ensconced in their offices, their gazes turned downward, q.a.-ing their own spreadsheets. They, too, were in the text. It's not that Cindy, Guy, the rest of the Quality Assurance Team, and I discoursed our days away, reading the author of that famous poststructuralist slogan "il n'y a pas de hors-texte," Jacques Derrida, because if we had, I would have enjoyed a sliver of recognition, some comfort of a reality confirmed and an expectation met.

I had studied the exemplary poststructuralist texts in college, classics from 1960s and '70s France like Luce Irigiray's gyno-linguistic *Speculum of the Other Woman* and Derrida's own verbal hall of mirrors, *Writing and Difference*. True, the seminars in which I'd read such treatises were wayward, free-associative affairs, ones that often revolved around a group of mildly stoned, non-French-speaking undergraduates being told by a professor that whatever word we had just devoted two and a half hours to contemplating—*jouissance*, for example—really couldn't be translated and was destined to dwell forever in the text. I can't say I took much from them, but I did grasp a certain ethical point, namely that language should be played with.

Derrida and his adherents to a purely textual world saw in it an irony and enjoyed an appreciable fun, an irreverence, even. You say this paper is a binding legal contact; the poststructuralist says no meaning is stable. You say money has worth because it represents exchangeable value; the poststructuralist says a dollar bill is a piece of paper with random markings on it. If you're going to be a poststructuralist, at least have fun with it. Like the time some friends of mine had matching soccer jerseys made that simply read "Poststructuralism" in place of a last name above their block of numbers. They wore these around Brooklyn's Prospect Park to the bemused look of those dogs and park goers versed in contemporary French theory. "The pleasure of the text," poststructuralists labeled their own approach, *le plaisir du texte*.

But the Arthur Andersen Quality Assurance Team didn't go in for textual *plaisir*. It was as though Guy had read Derrida, gotten 97 percent through it, but missed the 3 percent that contains the nod, the wink, the acknowledgment that sense and non-sense are one and the same. We had a textual process, not an experience of textual pleasure. The Process, it was called. Capitalized, always prefaced with that exclusive definite article "The," proper and proprietary, when a firm engaged Andersen in a consultancy project, they purchased The Process. Operating under the rubric of The Process conferred on businesses a certain immunity, probably because the regulatory agencies that judged immunity were themselves imprinted by the Big Five corporate accounting firms (after Andersen's criminal conviction, dissolution, and, still now, the Big Four), each of whom offered some version of The Process.

You say Y2K has the potential to be a global computer glitch that could shut down crucial nodes of modern infrastructure; The Process says our texts about Y2K will be glitch-free. Andersen wasn't about to risk selling a project that claimed to offer a Y2K fix—then Andersen itself could be sued. And the Conglomerate did not want to commit itself, whether contractually to its clients or in its filings with the Securities and Exchange Commission, to "fixing" something that may not have been fixable. From Andersen they bought legal deflection. And a lot of it. To get their money's worth, The Process insisted that we train our focus on things that could be written down, photocopied, and archived.

The advantage of the poststructuralist approach to Y2K was obvious enough to ascertain; it's easier to deal with an assemblage of verbiage than a techno-apocalypse. But I had witnessed, too, the risks of a world reduced to language. Two years before my corporate life began, the same French-inspired American academic world had been undone by the Sokal hoax, a bit in which physicist Alan Sokal wrote a fake article claiming that the power of language was stronger than that of gravity. He sent the article to a leading poststructuralist journal *Social Text*, where it was peer reviewed and published. Then he outed himself. He revealed in the pages of first *Lingua Franca* and ultimately the *New York Times* that he had submitted a compilation of nonsense, with a sprinkling of Heidegger and Newton, and in doing so had fooled some of the academy's leading literary scholars.

In 1998, the year of my Conglomerate hiring, Judith Butler had been named by journal *Philosophy and Literature* as one of the "most lamentable" writers of the year for their looping poststructuralist prose. By the late 1990s, academia's poststructuralists, scarred, it seems, by some understandable amount of trauma, began moving on to the greener pastures of German media studies and sociological theories of globalization, but not so the world of management consulting, whose commitment to the text was resolute. "Il n'y a pas de hors-texte" could have been printed on every team member's business card.

As the Quality Assurance Team scoured hundreds of thousands, millions even, of lines of Excel spreadsheets, we kept track of the textual problems we encountered. One inventory spreadsheet might list IBM PCs repeatedly, only to, out of nowhere, mention a single Dell device. We had a kind of weekly QA colloquium in which we presented our cases and debated the appropriate path forward: Had the mistake been in the original writing or in the copying? Imagine a scene of corporate hermeneuts scouring a text, returning to it for meanings shrouded, for interpretations yet undisturbed, for clues unbidden. The metaphor one reaches for is religious, the Bible, the Torah, the Koran. One could see Guy in the role of pope, with Cindy presiding over his Vatican council, busily distributing his various papal bulls and encyclicals; other QA Team members and the office writ large, a flock of lost laity waiting for divine direction. The problem with this analogy is that in each example there's an actual text. It need not be a bound book nor derive from a monotheistic tradition. The Buddha's final words—"things fall apart; tread the path with care" (so eerily appropriate to our Y2K setting)—would suffice here, too. But The Process seemed to have no printed home. To the extent that it existed, it passed somewhere between the minds and speech of Cindy and Guy, suspended in ethereal form. It was both accessible enough to be constantly appealed to—"The Process says," "According to The Process," "How would we apply The Process here?" "I'm not sure this syncs with The Process"—and inaccessible enough never to be grasped with Play-Doh–like tangibility.

With my philosophical background and atmospheric exposure to French—I had a secondary concentration in comparative literature, Modernist novels, especially—one might think I would have had an advantage over the engineers and business majors in matters textual and interpretative. And I did once reach my shaky hand into the poststructuralist bag of tricks to retrieve the old "this word negates its own meaning" bit, a Derridean favorite. At the inaugural meeting of the Cindy-spirited Database Oversight Committee, I gingerly pointed out that "oversight" was one of those rare antonymic nouns: it could mean either making mistakes or attending to them. I wondered if we might select a less ambivalent title for the committee. Some appreciable concern percolated in the cavernous conference room. Cindy promised to raise the issue with Guy. I was not privy to their discussions, but Cindy did return that Guy was comfortable with the word.

At a certain point, The Process meant not questioning The Process, and I had trouble locating exactly where that point was located. I had trouble fully embracing its logic, too; "Y2K is a documentation problem, not a technology problem." Did all team members believe this with the fidelity of Cindy? I scanned the office for signs of skepticism. A queer look from a team member that might indicate resignation or frustration, even bafflement or curiosity; all I saw was a sea of off-color blank miens, likely just the monitor tan that various team members, including me, had acquired as we attempted to secure the continuation of advertising into the next millennium.

Each working day brought us one day closer to our presumptive collective end, and, lest we forget, most team members had their own Y2K doomsday clock on their desk or mounted to the side of their cubicle, which tracked the years, months, days, hours, minutes, seconds, and milliseconds until techno-rapture. (That the times displayed weren't uniform produced a vertiginous effect all its own.) A bathroom break and a jaunt to the kitchenette to retrieve a Diet Pepsi nudged me three to four minutes closer to oblivion. Time advanced with a certain relentlessness, and yet most hours of most team members' days were devoted to copying inventories from spreadsheet to database or proofreading so-copied inventories. Work so dissociative and diminutive that, for me anyway, the need for bathroom breaks seemed increased in proportion to the amount of it I completed.

"Column 4, row 14: '18 routers' should be corrected to read '8 routers,'" my day began, as I compared database entry to inventory spreadsheet. I drafted this by hand, on my own spreadsheet. "Column 9, row 10, empty. Indicate yes or no," its penultimate moments included, on the same spreadsheet. The day's finale itself concerned not a text but its replica: the moment in which all Quality Assurance Analysts—not Cindy, for hierarchical reasons—convened in the photocopy room (more of a windowless corridor), wedged between men's room and kitchenette, to ensure that come what may on December 31, 1999, the deliverables from our day's labor would be preserved in perpetuity. Whatever moments of solidarity existed on the QA

Team sprouted in uncertain form between the blinding flashes and tray-clicks of that boxy Minolta copy machine—the only time we really spoke to each other in uncurated fashion—commuting woes, roommate dramas, awkward dates, student loan repayment plans, a rather unarticulated feeling of, what?

Cindy shepherded The Process and conducted random checks of all q.a.'ed spreadsheets. She kept the results in her own spreadsheet, a sort of master text. Guy and an elusive cabal of Andersen upper-tier management oversaw Cindy. Once, an Andersen partner, a rotund man named Benjamin, who wore a yarmulke, a three-piece suit, and those unfortunate slipper-like Merrell suede shoes just making their way into the world in the late 1990s, spent an hour in the office, presumably to q.a. Guy. Each of the Conglomerate's 1,100-plus agencies had submitted an initial technological inventory; they then supplied our Y2K office with any inventory amendments and updates. Those too had to be copied, checked, and cross-checked. We estimated that our team of four Quality Assurance Analysts could q.a. each inventory and document said q.a.-ing in six months, maybe longer. "On a project of this magnitude," Cindy explained at one of our QA colloquia, "I always say remember 'the three-thirds': it'll take 33 percent longer, cost 33 percent more, and be 33 percent more complex."

"Than what?" I hoped someone might ask. No one did.

After two months or so, and with an intensity and indeed desperation similar to that of my job hunt, I began something of a theoretical investigation. My question: Had I been unknowingly cast in a version of Charlie Chaplin's *Modern Times*, adapted for the information age and its possibly doomed conclusion, working title: *End Times*? Chaplin's rambunctious assembly line turned into a spreadsheet; the giant interlocking gears of industry rendered as towers of servers and routers, their flashing panels of green and red lights always indicating something or other; the film's final cut would reference Chaplin's *The Gold Rush* in which I would eat a Diet Pepsi can in place of the dapper Little Tramp eating a shoe. I despaired rather frequently and melodramatically, but I had not given up corporate hope. Indeed, to the extent that something was "amiss," as I vaguely narrated it to myself, to my girlfriend, to strangers at Brooklyn queer bars, I had to assume some of the fault—historically that had been the case. But a structural disadvantage must be noted and perhaps reconciled, too.

The Andersen people, my sort-of teammates, were always off attending this proprietary training or that, studying a proprietary report or at least carrying one around in a branded binder tucked under their arm. Did their cultured context make the work of quality assurance more interesting, or at least not corpse-level stultifying? Was there a proprietary route out of boredom so intense as to be experienced as dread? As a non-Andersen team member on an Andersen team, I would never know, but I did attempt to better myself, autodidact-style. I returned to a habit I had cultivated during my second (sadly, not first) year of college: reading. Frankly, getting through an issue of *Adweek* proved challenging: this account went here, that one went there; one campaign good, another bad, all kind of Dr. Seussian in narration. The *Wall Street Journal* I found more enjoyable: mid-caps and small caps; bullish and bearish; IRAs and 401(k)s; bonds versus stocks; the otherworldly appreciation of a real estate section that included descriptions of servants' quarters and a locale's tax-haven benefits. I even resuscitated a few items from the secondhand library I'd U-Hauled from Massachusetts to Brooklyn, where my brief foray in philosophy of technology seemed most germane. I was particularly drawn to philosopher Donna Haraway's 1997 book, one of the first to use internet grammar in its title, *Modest_Witness@Second_Millennium. FemaleMan©_Meets_OncoMouse*™, more for the novelty than for its content.[1] Finally, a theoretician who spoke to my predicament. But it wasn't a conversation.

Meanwhile, the Conglomerate's Y2K Managing Director, Justin, the apparent ACLU sympathizer with whom I'd spoken only briefly at my interview, had constructed a makeshift smoking lounge in the utility closet across the hall from my cubicle. It was there that he and Guy would liaise and swap status updates, I presumed. He often hosted suited visitors in that windowless walk-in humidor. If there were a corporate truth to be ascertained, the smoking lounge seemed a likely place for it to dwell. Were they meeting to discuss the same inventory spreadsheets as the QA Team's? To divine and implement The Process? To cross-check the database? Invariably these were older, suited white men. A world of Guys. I'd try to eavesdrop, of course, to attempt to pry bits of information from the clouds of secondhand smoke that escaped under the door and hovered momentarily about my cubicle before being absorbed into the carpet. A few gems did waft out. I learned, for example, that I wasn't the only team member to whom Cindy had described Arthur Andersen LLP as a pack of ravenous wolves: slender, agile, fangs bared, lips curled, marking their territory with urine—none of it meant pejoratively. When Justin heard this interspecies analogy, he balked. "More like bloodsucking leeches. They overcharge. Bullshit their billable hours. They want my employees to fuck up so I'll fire them, and they can bring in more Andersen people... [*inaudible*] Of course they're part of our team."

But what, really, was there to hear? That The Process was vertically integrated apocrypha? That Guy had knowledge of his firm's fraudulent endeavors at Enron and WorldCom and was perpetuating something similar here? That the link between signifier and signified, word and its material referent, was every bit as random as the poststructuralists insisted? No such claims circulated in the office, none participated in our discourse, none were strictly, or even broadly, speaking true. In fact, Guy and Cindy could not have been more faithful, devoted as they were to channeling The Process to the larger office: the managers, the regular analysts, the data entry temps, the database team, the circulating "roving analysts." "Y2K is a documentation problem, not a technology problem," Cindy recanted at our weekly Analysts Meetings and invited us to repeat after her. Once more, with feeling, "Y2K is a documentation problem, not a technology problem."

Rather, the fact of the matter—if the situation had facts or matter, both debatable—was that the Y2K bug possessed a certain latitude. Would we all be launched *Back to the Future*–like into a new stone age on 1/1/2000 or, conversely, would a few rest-area vending machines conk out and everyone would get on with it? Of course, one had to assume the worst, but that's quite a spread of possibility. The Y2K project that Andersen designed for and sold to the Conglomerate had to contend with these variables. Such latitude cut both ways; it allowed some freedoms, like recasting the entire affair as a spreadsheet, as it induced other anxieties. About how many multimillion-dollar management consulting projects could one reasonably claim: *This is actually fake?*

Yet if history's record attests to anything, it's that millennial transitions unsettle humans, make them liable to do and believe strange things. There was the year 1—but no year 0, a bug in Western recordkeeping, and perhaps a premonition—with the initiation of a so-called Common Era, whose claims to "commonness" seem a bit overstated since the whole epoch is anchored by a splintering event whose effects still linger today: Did God send his son to earth to suffer, die, and undergo resurrection or not? Then 999 became 1000, and millenarians were afoot throughout Europe. They proclaimed their own truths from divine poverty to vegetarianism and were met with the wrath of kings and feudal lords. That first millennial transition, too, had exhibited definite oddities: monsters dot official historical records as do marauding crusaders, witch trials, and public burnings, and while the label "Dark Ages" has been retired, one can somewhat sympathize with its progenitors.

Now the 1000s were poised to become a 2000. Or one could hope, anyway, and in place of religion-inflected world endings and beginnings, denizens of global modernity were faced with a computerized eschatology: late second-millennial humans unintentionally had included an on/off switch in their civilization's infrastructure and even more unintentionally had set it to flip to "off" on 1/1/2000. Throughout the late 1980s and early '90s, a few soothsayers had been bruiting tales of this second and most unwelcome coming around congressional halls, regulatory agencies, professional associations, survivalist group meetings, to the point that, finally, some were heard. One alert in particular, that three-page article in *Computerworld* titled "Doomsday 2000" that later become a book of the same name, written by prognosticator Peter de Jager and published in 1993, was donned "the information-age equivalent of the midnight ride of Paul Revere" by the *New York Times*. Listen, my children, and you shall hear of the millennial ride of Pete Jager. Soon thereafter, the US secretary of defense suggested that Y2K amounted to "the electronic equivalent of the El Niño." And soon after that, management consulting firms began selling Y2K-preparedness packages to their Fortune 500 clients—if the situation couldn't be definitively remedied, at least a kind of corporate cordon sanitaire could be put in place.

Learning what exactly constituted that boundary allowed me to cross, or at least get a glimpse of, the textual threshold I sought. Several months into my employment, in mid-November '98, so appeared the Executive Council Meeting. Some of the Andersen and Conglomerate elite visited our Y2K office to see what a $4 million (the price I had heard bandied about) purchase of the Andersen project had produced in terms of Y2K preparedness: CEOs, COOs, CFOs, CTOs, an alphabet of executives, some with aides-de-camp, filed through our office. White men in their fifties and sixties, in dark suits, walking slowly and seldom speaking, an almost funeral procession. They were similarly somber on their way out—only an hour on each team member's doomsday clock had elapsed. Soon after their departure, Managing Director Justin invited all team members into the conference room, where a Roman banquet of muffins and fruit pyramids, a well-appointed coffee cart, and an assortment of Pepsi products greeted us. None of the provisions had been touched, and team members were invited to pick through the council's refuse. "We just had over one hundred million dollars' worth of executives in here," Justin began, "and they wanted updates."

"Il n'y a pas de hors-texte" | 41

Team members were encouraged to review for themselves a paper copy of the Executive Council Presentation, many of which lay scattered about the thirty-foot oblong conference table. I was rather perplexed to see that it was essentially a rehash of the New Hire Presentation. The cartoon duck holding the sledgehammer. The stick figure wondering, "On January 1, 2000, will I still have . . . ?" The floating text box, conceptual art-like in display, "Y2K is a documentation problem, not a technology problem." But the presentation's contents were overshadowed by the mood emitting from the all-male managerial cadre; ebullient and self-assured, it commanded the conference room. Even the always starched and monogramed Guy looked pleased. The man seldom spoke outside of closed-door klatches, which only increased the sagacious air about him. As a measure of the morning's importance, he was invited by Justin to address the team.

He rose and delivered a brief litigious soliloquy:

```
When January first of the year 2000
hits and a floodgate of Y2K lawsuits
descends, and [we're] being sued
by everyone, and the firms who
aren't suing us, we're suing, the
indemnification issues, the claims
of fiduciary responsibility, and
accusations of abandonment thereof.
What are we going to need? Proof.
They're going to want to know what
we did and how we did it. So that's
what this council is concerned
with, proof, paper, documentation.
```

> And that's why our battle plan is simple: keep documenting, team."

Team members nodded in recognition of Guy's wisdom but also, I think, in recognition of our own collective efforts—guided by The Process, we were traveling the right path. Justin offered more distinction by way of summary. "The point is the council was impressed. With this whole office. Every team member is important. So are your families."

Write What You Know

Some quarter of a century later, I feel confident in my use of quotations and in my recollection of things like the pyramidal arrangement of a fruit platter or the price tag on the muffin tray at the Executive Council Meeting because, by that point in my corporate life, about three months in, I had begun keeping my own records. It wasn't my idea but an offshoot of our office mantra, "Y2K is a documentation problem, not a technology problem." If that were the case, and the Andersen people claimed daily that it indeed was, then not only would the Quality Assurance Team have to manage the documenting of all the Conglomerate's technological holdings—which we indeed were—but team members would need to have their own documentation, too.

The Process encouraged it. "Cover Your Ass," team members with more seniority than I possessed had often advised me in the casual moments any office offers—an unexpected elevator ride together, a chance encounter in the linoleum-covered kitchenette, an awkward bathroom exchange. "Write everything down," they suggested. If the most terrific of Y2K predictions arrived, even if only some of the more banal ones were realized, we'd likely all find ourselves as defendants in some protracted bout of corporate litigation; the lowest ranks among us would be sacrificed, that's always the way of it. A captain may go down with his ship, but

| 43

a CEO glides away on a golden parachute while his company implodes. Look no further than the CEO of the *Titanic*'s parent company, the White Star Line, who, riding on that ship's doomed maiden voyage, had leapt aboard one of its precious few lifeboats. I'd then be legally vulnerable, save my own documentation.

The first time I heard this anxious Fortune 500 fantasy unspooled, it seemed so contingent and otherworldly—me? on trial? for fiduciary abdication? I didn't even have a savings account—that I dismissed it as an urban legend, Midtown-style. But so many team members, in so many unique positions, with different personalities, to say nothing of varying risk exposures, had reiterated a version of the scenario that I had to accept it had some basis in our shared transactional reality. I started writing. This is the way the world ends.

Picayune observations, dialogue transcriptions, org chart descriptions, status report summaries, agendas, I was now taking notes, sometimes in an official capacity and other times as a private citizen. Like at the ambivalently named Database Oversight Committee, for example. In fact, so compromised was its mission that the committee met only once before being dissolved. Its ill-fated inaugural congress transpired on a mid-October Wednesday at 5:00 p.m. A mix of Andersen people and Conglomerate employees, including two database programmers, a network analyst, a business analyst, Quality Assurance members, and the Managing Director, it unfolded in rather halting fashion.

```
Justin: OK, we got everybody? I
don't think anyone needs a reminder
of the importance of database
```

oversight. No one's leaving this room until we have a plan.

Cindy: Well, two people are leaving because they made it clear they had prior commitments at 6 p.m. and the meeting was thirty minutes late starting.

Justin: Fine. Two people. But no one else. Who's taking notes?

Cindy: Leigh Claire is. Any questions, Leigh Claire, before we start?

Leigh Claire: The committee's name. Oversight? It could mean to overlook something instead of to oversee it. Maybe a new name would be better?

Cindy: We'll punt that to Guy and circle back. Let's get started.

Snippets such as these, I recorded and put in a binder. Soon, the mimetic posture of my prose became narrativized and started to occupy a somewhat enjoyable part of my working day. I had, for another example, captured the scene before the council's convening.

The Executive Council meets today.
I'm nervous and I don't even
understand what exactly it is.
But it's certainly of paramount
importance. The whole office is in
a collective tizzy, everything and
everybody metamorphosing to be
Executive-Council ready. Earlier in
the week a professional cleaning
crew wearing white jumpsuits arrived
and vacuumed everything including
the walls. All team members have
been asked to abandon our [sic]
usual business casual wear in favor
of business formal, meaning a suit
or something resembling a suit. It
looks like everyone has complied,
not that it matters. Non-Council-
attending team members have been
told not to leave their seats during
the meeting, even though the meeting
is a closed-door, conference-room
hosted event. Non-Council-attending
team members have also been asked
to avoid talking to any one of the
Council attendees. That shouldn't
be too difficult since the Council
will parade in, turn left at the
receptionist's cubicle, and beeline
to the conference room.

My discrete predictions of corporate choreography had been accurate. But more importantly, my focus, geared as it was toward comportment, sartorial display, circulation through the office, had been the appropriate one. I was slowly but surely starting to intuit the logic that undergirded The Process. By convening such an elite roster, the Conglomerate had signaled to all who might be preparing a Y2K lawsuit against it that preparations were being taken seriously at its highest echelons. A certain satisfaction accompanied my realization, as did a certain disappointment. It had been thrilling to glimpse the content of the Executive Council Presentation, to sit where they'd sat, to see what they had seen. At the same time, what I saw was that the Executive Council was just as immersed in duck cartoons and stick figures as were the new hires.

That's when I expanded my writerly repository to include more idiosyncratic thoughts and fleeting impressions, like little character studies of my colleagues. In fact, that's when I began to have the vaguest of premonitions that my life's path lay in writing about corporate quality assurance instead of undertaking it. In my original text's originary moments I stood, let us say, faced with two possible truths, both discomfiting in their implications. The first one, grand: that corporate capitalism is something of a charade. The second, less totalizing but more despairing, at a personal level, at least: that I had a data entry position on a fake project with largely but not wholly insufferable coworkers. At that moment of initial reveal, so unrehearsed was I on the corporate and conceptual stage, that I simply could not behold either claim with the concentration it deserved.

So I did what writers do. I wrote what I knew. No doubt the result of years of reading poststructuralism, my early reminiscences of my businessman life display a singular focus on gender as it organized both the corporate hierarchy and sense of belonging therein. Before my successful placement by Careers by Penthouse, I had visited another employment agency called Mademoiselle—both, I suggested in my budding text, sounded like names of a westside gentleman's club. At Mademoiselle, I'd met the woman who I had to suppose was the Madam and who instructed me to wear suits composed of skirts rather than pants. "And remember, honey, that means above the knee. Employers want to see legs." Despite her advice and my compliance, our collaboration did not land me a job or her a commission.

I noted the distribution of titles and nicknames at the Conglomerate. Cindy was referred to as "the den mother"—she was in her late twenties. Guy had a title that recognized his central place: "Guy, the Documentation Expert." Justin, our commander, was hailed as "the General." I, along with another young woman and Quality Assurance Analyst, an Ivy-plus engineer by training who shared my hair color, had bestowed on us the clunky moniker "the blonde QA twins." As we walked the office lap to the photocopier together every afternoon, team members would exclaim in a strangely exaggerated fashion, "Hey—there go the blonde QA twins" and "Am I seeing double or is it the blonde QA twins?"

I documented the gender division of weekly events. Tuesday's Analysts' Meetings were all-female affairs; Monday's Managers Meetings were phallic palavers. (Team members reminisced about a certain female Conglomerate higher-up at a different office who used to invite underlings via the all-office intercom to "strap on a pair of balls and come see me.") Wednesday's General Meetings had all the grace of a middle school dance, where the sexes mixed and codes of gendered performance were rehearsed and solidified. Andersen's corporate motto declared: "Think Straight, Talk Straight," and the firm's commitment to heteronormativity showed; it inflected, too, the typically less straight advertising culture at the Conglomerate.

I kept these growing corporate impressions in one of my cubicle's many binders. This one was, like the rest of them, white and three-ring, but its title, running down its laminated spine, stood out from bangers like "Inventories," "Quality Assurance," and "Documentation." This binder, my own existential compendium, I baptized as "Bildungsroman." It seemed appropriate—I was coming of age, but so was global modernity, and we were both destined to encounter a world-changing, if not world-ending, event, Y2K, one that deserved an account and one that I was in the surprising position to give. When a new, originally from Vienna team member, who had been hired to prepare for Phase II and who understood the German vocabulary if not the meaning of the phrase "Bildungsroman," inquired as to why I had an "education novel" in my cubicle, I explained to her that these were personal documents, memorial documents, reactions to an amateur corporate life, and that the title was "kind of ironic." She didn't respond, so I continued, "Like, what do we learn here? I mean if this were a novel?" She wasn't familiar with the bildungsroman genre, so the joke, not that funny to begin with, was, in any case, lost in translation (even though the translation was correct).

The humor seemed so obvious to me. My Bildungsroman was assuredly not a novel, nothing fictional about it. Its contents indexed an actual human existence, mine. To stress the nonfictional nature of my writerly enterprise, I gave it a documentary-like subtitle, "Bildungsroman: A Year in My Life." In between q.a.-ing spreadsheets and photocopying them, I had somehow developed a plan to recount and stylize real-life corporate scenes in the most extraordinary of circumstances, namely staring down the barrel of an oncoming apocalypse. That nonfiction detail aside, however, my intent was to follow the usual conventions of the bildungsroman genre and to trace a youthful subject, me, developing an idiosyncratic yet nonetheless generalizable awareness of the modern world and her place in it. I'd make only necessary substitutions. Like corporate managers in place of a nuclear family, and corporate team members in place of a circle of friends. Every Bildungsroman, every coming-of-age story, needs a sidekick, someone to draw out the protagonist, someone with whom passion and dispassion can be shared if not consummated, someone to benchmark narrative and historical progress, and that's how Viennese Magdalena—Leni, the German diminutive—entered mine.

Honestly, I couldn't have conjured more of a character had I tried: tall and thin, accented and bespectacled, she hailed from fallen Austrian nobility. Her family had lost seven-eighths of their estate after World War I, but they nonetheless remained comfortable enough not to have to concern themselves with bourgeois trifles, like work or mortgages. Had her father fought with the Nazis? Indeed, he had. Imagine a Captain von Trapp-like personality who had never softened under the melodious ensorcellment of a Fraulein Maria. But there end any *The Sound of Music* parallels, and Leni fled her father's eastern Reich not by waltzing and yodeling her way over the Alps but through an American husband who helped her get a green card, then through a transnational law firm that got her experience, then by a visit to the Careers by Penthouse employment agency, and, finally, via an analyst position at the Conglomerate. When she interviewed with Guy, she had been asked to rate her foreign language abilities on a scale of one to ten. Fluent in German, English, and French, proficient in Spanish, able to make her way through a Latin text with a pocket dictionary, she had given herself a ten.

"Bildungsroman: A Year in My Life," that's the title of my first, still unpublished, book. My manuscript in permanent waiting, if you will. Its most spectacular scenes featured Leni. Like the time she unwittingly hijacked a certain Wednesday's General Meeting and sent The Process into momentary disarray. Or our explorations of the ideal ratio of work to pleasure while drunk on a Greek beach during one international Y2K-oriented business trip. Then there was the time we almost died, or at least had occasion to consider our immediate mortality, when our taxi caught fire in Mexico City.

If there are any business or labor archives accepting donations dated from the 1990s, I'd gladly fork over the original text. I actually did compose the majority of it during those twelve looming fin-de-siècle months of 1999 while employed at the Conglomerate. As a master's thesis, perhaps for a narrative nonfiction MFA, it's OK. Were I to grade it today, I'd give it a B-. Strong on ambition, real creative vision and energy; far too many unhinged narrative throughlines, uneven in tone and pace, saturated with unintended private associations. I needed an editor!

But I also needed a point. Because every writer who intends to write what she knows will eventually encounter something she doesn't know, and in my case, that unknown was capitalism. Of course, I understood that the historical scene generally was capitalist, that it formed our basic economic orientation. Likewise, I knew the Conglomerate was a for-profit entity, as were most of the franchises I passed on my four-block walk to and from the Rockefeller Center subway stop to Fifty-Fourth Street each day. I tried while writing that initial draft of my Bildungsroman to consider the big economic picture, aware, as I was, that the broader and more convincing my portrait of corporate capitalism, the more clearly this particular business absurdity—my career—would come into sharp relief.

But there, on the twenty-fourth floor of that Midtown skyscraper, amidst the whirl of capital's millennial circulation, I became only dizzy. Too bad my recently purchased critical thinking apparatus—those four years at Hampshire "College" hadn't come cheap—didn't prove to be the asset I needed to decipher my political economic surrounds; if anything, it prepared me to glean a superficial and self-satisfied understanding. I could construct a philosophical analogy for most of what I encountered at the Conglomerate, and I did, but it never occurred to me to question on what ground such analogies stood. Day after day, week after week, month after month of reading and populating spreadsheets transformed me into something spreadsheet-like myself: capacious but concept-less, able to record, to list, to organize and sort, but according to an unthought, unthinkable orientation.

Nor would months more of quality assurance labor offer what I needed to produce a concept to anchor my Bildungsroman. No, I first located what was required to make sense of all this several years after my corporate tenure (and not modern technology) had ended, when I attempted Karl Marx's doorstopper of a treatise, *Capital*, volume 1. At the time I undertook that first reading, my days at the Conglomerate had well passed, my PhD study had begun, and I was taking a semester's long course on volume 1, first page to last. Meanwhile, my Bildungsroman had sedimented into one of those albatross-like works in progress in which the progress part becomes more and more difficult to ascertain, particularly in proportion to the work part. I had enrolled in graduate school in part to finish the damn thing, but one year of PhD coursework had left me more confused, not less, and any long-sought point I needed to truly finish writing my first book remained elusive.

So there I was, preparing to walk away from the unfinished reminisces of my businessman days, when a certain socialist phrase fairly arrested me. A hundred pages or so into *Capital* with crucial, if tortuously difficult, definitions arrived at and first principles settled, Marx invites his audience to suspend their perception of daily economic activity and to "take leave for a time of this noisy sphere, where everything takes place on the surface and in view of all men." The passage grabs most readers with such force—just for its clarity if nothing else—so in that I was hardly unique. But I like to think I was distinguished among my *Capital*-reading confrères by the analogue I conjured.

Because, although two years had passed, I was transported back to the twenty-fourth floor of the Conglomerate's Midtown skyscraper: the receptionist's radio, the meandering men, my own lack of privacy in the cubicle. I realized that while working at the Conglomerate, I had sat daily in that cacophonous sphere, the very place Marx suggests investigators must leave to follow capitalists "into the hidden abode of production, on whose threshold there stares us in the face 'No admittance except on business.'"[1] The Conglomerate's Y2K office, too, had contained such a threshold: the managerial smoking lounge on whose door a warning duly appeared. It declared "Do Not Enter."

Hastily taped and unlevel, more appropriate for a child's clubhouse, really, it was still sturdy enough to withstand its hinged host being slammed multiple times daily. "Goddammit, get me Guy," Justin would bark at the receptionist as he passed in front of my cubicle, flung open the door, lit a cigarette, and yanked it shut—all a seamless motion. The receptionist would just as quickly broadcast through the all-office intercom, "Guy, pick up line one. Guy, line one. Guy is on line one."

Don't lose the trail, Marx encourages. Only if one perseveres, only if one becomes a detective of capitalism, so to speak, only then, one "shall see, not only how capital produces, but how capital is produced. We shall at last force the secret of profit making."[2] Before working at the Conglomerate, I hadn't wanted to force any such secret. I wasn't even aware that one existed. But once there, it didn't take long for me to become as convinced as a Southern evangelist that forces stronger than Cindy and Guy were exerting their pull; that something larger than Arthur Andersen's Process or the Conglomerate's devotion to brand loyalty lingered in our midst, that some kind of *secret*—I wouldn't have used that word—had been operating.

On that first semester-long and, honestly, rather uncomfortable acquaintance with Marx, I was unaware that his work and more done in his legacy had the potential to resuscitate my Bildungsroman, to let me complete it, finally, by supplying what had always been absent, namely an understanding of capitalism, its labor practices in particular. But what I did recognize, almost instantaneously, was that some of the initial questions "Bildungsroman: A Year in My Life" had explored as though it were broaching a new theoretical frontier had already been answered. For example, what was it like to be a Guy? A Justin? To move in their habitus? To reside in their *umwelt*? Marx had addressed this personage, even if tangentially and somewhat dismissively: "His soul is the soul of capital," Marx writes, not of Guy himself, obviously, but of the capitalist, who, Marx continues, "is only capital personified."[3] True, but those personifications take different forms.

Although in his mid-thirties, Justin lumbered about the office, often noticeably short of breath. Sometimes he used a cane to assist him as he traveled from his corner office to the managerial smoking lounge, a carpeted distance of probably twenty-five feet. He was rash, loud, and exuberant, but he could read people and relate to them on what he thought was a personal level; the two times we spoke casually he included an out-of-context but good word about the ACLU. Once, in that dead winter December, as 1998 beckoned 1999, the opening crackle of the all-office intercom gave way not to an announcement, per usual, but to Justin playing *The Brady Bunch* theme song?! Team members, me included, laughed in surprise and relief, alone in our cubicles and offices, but somehow in concert nonetheless. Think of Justin as a cross between Tony Soprano and my father. The former, a large, endearing sociopath with an aptitude for business and an appetite for food. My father, of shorter stature but identical body type, balding pattern, and Italian heritage, was likewise possessed of a ludic bon vivant energy. A failed early modern English historian turned academic administrator, the man could have been more empathetic, even if that lack hardly reached a level of murderous sociopathy. Dad, too, loved to eat as well as to transact, but his business acumen was so underdeveloped that at his funeral, my partner accurately eulogized him, and this allowing for the generosity afforded during mourning, as "on the wrong end of every boondoggle." Mourners laughed in recognition.

Guy appeared more sprightly yet more advanced in age, at least by two decades. Gray and distinguished, calm and obsequious, he wore only black wingtips. He worked for Justin, kind of. After all, it was the Conglomerate that contracted with Andersen to design and administer its Y2K project, and to Justin he deferred (not in the Derridean sense, but as the colloquially used English verb would have it: to give way). Guy didn't smoke or drink or, it turns out, really eat. Takeout orders arrived on the twenty-fourth floor throughout the day, and by late afternoon many team members' desks resembled one of those detritus-strewn stretches of beach after a particularly violent storm. But not Guy's, whose desktop's "Gone Golfing" figurine I never saw once obscured by waxed deli-wrappings or emptied fried rice cartons. An ascetic, a corporate bodhisattva, he'd emerge from a conclave in the managerial smoking lounge, about the size of an airplane lavatory but lacking the latter's ventilation, ashen-faced and red-eyed but steely and resolute, nonetheless: fiduciary duty must be done. But then in another way, Justin worked for Guy. Recall the old banking aphorism—I always forget whether Keynes or Stalin said it—that if you owe a bank one hundred bucks, they control you. But if you owe a million, you control them. Guy could deliver a robust project, or not. He could recycle compromising information about Justin to Conglomerate higher-ups, or not. Modern technology could conclude on 12/31/1999, or it could continue. Things could go one way, or they could go another.

As could have my Bildungsroman. I might have at some point declared it either done or dead. Instead, I lived with it for twenty-some-odd years as one might knowledge of an estranged relative.

They are out there, somewhere. One knows of their existence as something of an uncomfortable truth, and with each passing year opportunities for encounter recede, but they don't fully disappear. Nor did my text. "The tradition of all the dead generations weighs like a nightmare on the brain of the living," Marx wrote of French political history in the wake of the French Revolution.[4] I can confirm that one's own unfinished book exerts a similar effect.

Which is why I've decided to return to it (again), and this time to lower the casket into the grave. To write what I *now* know. If the first version of my Bildungsroman, the original one, collected assorted corporate hijinks, delighted in managerial pleonasms, pointed out, and rightly so, that consulting and most white-collar work is appropriative at best and criminal at worst, then this version probes what it meant for me to critique corporate work in late capitalism without a concept of corporate work or late capitalism. One can do it, that I proved, but one finds oneself and one's story quickly wanting. So this version makes amendments and rights the course.

This version has a new name, too: *Fake Work*. I was certainly doing something during my employ at the Conglomerate, as were the Andersen people and the other Conglomerate team members, but the precise nature of our tasks requires further investigation. The world doesn't need another *Capital*, and even if it did, I couldn't author it. But I can attend to a certain lost moment in time, an event, Y2K, a fictitious crisis, which demands its own set of critical and, now it seems, personal questions, too. I can attend to the present as well, which is necessarily different from the past, even if no philosopher has ever been able to determine the precise moment that one becomes the other.

Teamwork

While I'm today something of a well-known meeting loather, during my Fortune 500 days, I embraced them and did so genuinely. If one began at 1:00 p.m., I arrived in the conference room by 12:55. "Don't want to be late," I might explain. To myself. Or, "Gotta have time to preview the agenda." Actually, meetings held the one opportunity I had for human connection between 9:00 a.m. and 5:00 p.m., 8:15 a.m. and 5:45 p.m. if we count the commute, and I savored every minute of them. From the table of the conference room, I'd gaze at a vista beyond that of an inventory spreadsheet. I'd luxuriate in the chance to observe team members in their native corporate settings, and sometimes even speak to them. Sure, the food delivery people regularly mistook me for the receptionist, so close were our Formica cubicles, but pointing someone and their stapled bag of food cartons to the right or left or telling them that the actual receptionist was in the kitchenette didn't offer the social engagement I required to endure the textual isolation demanded by quality assurance work. Meetings did. They reminded me of the bigger issue, Y2K, of the fact that I was employed for a bigger entity, the Conglomerate, of the fact that it produced ads—"See the new iMac subway posters?" one team member might comment to another before a meeting's start. And I anticipated none more than the General Meeting.

It occurred each Wednesday at 2:00 p.m., a perfect bisection of the working week. All forty or so team members attended: the chummy database programmers, who never spoke, the disheveled but crucial IT coterie, the Andersen people, four Conglomerate managers and their four analysts, the Media Team, the third-party partners team, Guy; sometimes the receptionist even set the phone to an automated answer function and popped by. By January 1999 the General Meeting's coordinates had begun to feel expected and reassuring: at 2:00 p.m., everyone except Justin was seated in the conference room, Pepsi product in one hand, Cindy-authored agenda in the other, waiting for the meeting's commencement, at which point Justin would announce through the all-office intercom that the meeting would begin five minutes late. Those minutes passed; he trudged in, a cloud of cigarette smoke all but trailing him, took hold of the agenda, and said, "All right team, what did we get done this week?"

The routine proceeded as if choreographed, which by some definitions I suppose it was, by Cindy. Last week's Upcoming Tasks had been moved to this week's Completed Tasks, save the Ongoing Tasks section. This week's Upcoming Tasks, in turn, became next week's Completed Tasks, a rotation that would proceed until 12/31/1999. What this meant, among other things, was that the agenda itself was somewhat useless, and it seemed to be its destiny to be recycled into the one truly participatory part of the General Meeting, the anonymous "What's Good? What Needs Improving?" all-team exercise. Team members were instructed to rip a piece off some desolate corner of their 8.5-by-11 agenda and compose two reflections in accord with the title. The compositions were then passed to the table's head for Justin to read aloud. Cindy often emphasized that on a project like ours, one marked by both its complexity and duration, team members' morale, their sense of inclusion and spiritual buy-in, all of which could be strengthened through participation in collective endeavors, might well be the pivot on which success turned.

A sense of collective recognition wasn't the only reason, of course. The meetings, their agendas, the "What's Good? What Needs Improving?" go-round and the documentation of the foregoing, these were all required by The Process. If a Y2K event did occur and the Conglomerate was unable to place a contractually agreed-on advertisement and a lawsuit resulted, our archive of meetings would be yet another buttress to support the Conglomerate's defense. The fact that team members had been encouraged to criticize and offered a public avenue to seek team betterment would likely be seen as signs of a professional, aware, and self-actualizing office.

That said, any content produced through the exercise had become rather generic. "What's Good: working like a team"; "Needs improving: kitchen out of Sweet'N Low" one anonymous team member's comments might declare. "What's Good: getting a lot done;" "Needs Improving: printer 2 won't print double-sided," advised another. To such discrete problems, Justin responded discreetly: "Whoever is having printer problems should ask Matt [IT guy] for help"; "Whoever wants more Sweet'N Low should ask Yolie [office manager] to place an order." In the event that the author, or anyone else, for that matter, let their attention lapse during Justin's recitation-response and missed some bit of office knowledge, Cindy was there, court stenographer–like in accuracy, taking notes, whose dissemination one could expect not ten minutes after the meeting's end.

But even the most conscientious notetakers have lapses and make elisions. Because as one particular General Meeting seemed headed toward conclusion, an event occurred that was not only unscripted by Cindy but which she elected not to record in the official documentation. It was a kind of volcanic eruption into "What's Good? What Needs Improving?" Yet a volcano allows warnings, little quakes and gaseous emissions precede the explosion. Not so in the conference room; this top just blew. Justin was reading aloud from the shrinking pile of team members' comments, and he began a new set of comments with a fundamentally unassuming entry. "What's Good: enjoyed my office Secret Santa Gift." Lucky team member, I thought. I'd been gifted a three-inch-tall plastic paper-clip cartoon character, one with huge bulging eyes and dangling arms and one that I then felt pressured to display since it'd been a present from someone who likely passed by my cubicle daily.

Justin continued reading, "Needs Improving: I don't understand what the Media Team does and I will not accept 'ask a member of the Media Team' for an answer." As he enunciated, Justin's countenance shifted from one of initial curiosity to that of uncertain disdain. He became aware—as did all team members—that his managerial style, his habit of passing requests on to others, was being subtly mocked. Not only that: his antagonist was sitting amongst us, cloaked in a veil of anonymity. With a sly smile, a presentation somewhere between intrigued and embarrassed, he asked, "Who wrote this?" That query caused a swift reaction in Cindy, who one felt at the level of basic character, to say nothing of commitment to The Process, needed to respond. "This is an anonymous exercise," she began, and no doubt had more to say before Justin interrupted her: "Thank you, Cindy." So chastened, Cindy let Justin continue: "I asked," he repeated, "who wrote this?"

Dead silence. The urban kind only a skyscraper can provide, where a soft machinic din emits from the building itself. At that moment one hears no wind, no sirens, no honking or beeping, none of the dissonance that one knows swirls street level, twenty-four stories below. A nervous calm settled over the conference room, and team members, careful to avoid potentially implicating eye contact with one another, fixed their downcast stares on their Pepsi beverages, diet ones and those with a full calorie count. Pepsi had just purchased Snapple, so there were a few of its high-octane iced tea bottles about, too. Justin read the room's quiet as opposition, not as the submission it surely was, and rather than relent, he intensified his inquisition. "You don't want to tell me? Fine. We'll sit here all goddamn day. We'll sit here till Y2K. Because I'm going to find out who wrote this fucking note." Then a dramatic pause, followed by his concluding direction: "No one is leaving this room until I do."

Aside from the rare but intense discussions of whether the world and humanity with it would indeed perish in a matter of months, this was an unmatched piece of office drama whose culmination was undoubtedly the detectivity provided by heretofore-unmentioned female Andersen person, Tracy. Sitting to the right of Cindy, usually an unremarkable seat selection, she reached over, took the offending paper scrap, and meekly announced to the nervous audience: "It's a girl's handwriting." As juvenile as it sounds, I couldn't have felt more relieved. My script is scraggly, disorganized, and angular, the furthest thing from that of a girl's. Tracy, too, must have felt some relief: one couldn't help but notice that she had just exculpated herself. And

Cindy, who would suspect her? As team members began silently scanning those seated around the conference table, privately searching for someone whose handwriting was bubbly and who menstruated, the silence broke.

"I did it—I wrote the note." Leni! Daughter of a Nazi! (Not a party member, but an infantryman, her father had been of some advanced age when she was born.) A feeling of simultaneous relief, among female team members, and disbelief, among all team members, was palpable. Leni had only been in the office for a month or so. And as managing Y2K director, Justin no doubt had signed off on her hiring, but now, as he stared at her, I wondered if he even remembered her name. She herself had more to say, and did so in somewhat halting fashion. "It's just that you never answer questions, and I thought, well, I thought, you're the boss, you will know." As I had caught her attention with my desktop "Bildungsroman" binder, she had caught mine with her performance piece.

Once something of an office friendship had solidified between us, I asked her what Justin had said to her in private—he'd ended the meeting by ordering her to stay alone with him in the conference room. "That I'm on his 'shit list,'" she told me. And what did she say? "Fine." My sympathy was immediate. I could have been her. In most of life's moments, I would have been her, and had I not devoted myself to not being her for reasons of corporate compliance, I would have been her right then and there. Had it ever occurred to me to use the anonymity of the "What's Good" exercise to make untoward remarks—"What's Good: use of Play-Doh on QA Team continues to bear fruit"; "Needs Improving: I may be depressed"—I fought the urge weekly. But I had promised myself: my time at the Conglomerate will not meet the same sorry end that my teenaged travails at Taco Bell had.

And perhaps I wasn't the only one sparring with psychoanalytic demons. What of the strange duel Leni had provoked with Justin: this was our General? The man to deliver the Conglomerate to the other side of history on January 1, 2000? His tantrum seemed to require an explanation, and team members provided one to each other in hushed tones while shuffling about the kitchenette after the General Meeting's denouement: that the stress had gotten to him; that no one man should be tasked with the fate of advertising after the dawn of the third millennium; that anonymity had no place in a Fortune 500 office.

In fact, the Media Team—never did Leni or anyone else for that matter receive a public explanation as to what it did—was the next stop in my ersatz Andersen rotation, but I had no idea such a future awaited me. What I did know was that as those early months of 1999 advanced, Phase I: Inventory was, thankfully, desperately, finally, concluding. Phase II would require a more cosmopolitan presentation of our team because we would be conducting Y2K site visits on a global scale to match the Conglomerate's geographical reach—that's part of the reason trilingual Leni had come on board. The Quality Assurance Team would continue to be crucial, as the site visits had to be documented and the documentation checked. Team members would soon be bound for Sydney and Hong Kong, Dusseldorf and Paris.

I myself had been dispatched to the slightly less glamorous destination of Dallas, Texas, location of one of the Conglomerate's key stateside shops. It made no difference. To me, Dallas might well have been Hong Kong, foreign and dreamlike. Texas would deliver me to a new world. For two days, I would be outside of my cubicle, without the spreadsheets, divorced from the database. This would be a conceptual journey, too, from signifier to signified—finally, a chance to encounter something real, an avenue to carry me beyond the text. It wasn't only that I'd never been to an advertising agency, I'd never even been inside of an office building other than the one in which I now worked. I wore a suit. On the plane.

I rendezvoused at the car rental counter in the Dallas airport with the two other members of my site-visit crew—another female analyst with whom I was friendly and a male Andersen manager whom I'd heard spoken of in glowing terms in various meetings but had never met—and soon the three of us were in a hearse-sized white Cadillac cruising through a corporate park large enough to require multiple zip codes. The make and model of car were the result of an upgrade, the Andersen manager, Darren L., explained. He had recently achieved colonel rank in the car rental agency's loyalty program, and this was his first dividend, a kind of automotive epaulet to announce his stature.

As often happens when traveling over space, from the Northeast to Texas, our trip became a kind of time travel, too, and in our case, we arrived into a world of 1980s television. Network drama references had begun on the journey from the airport to the Four Seasons Hotel and Resort. "God, I miss Dallas," female analyst Barbara commented as we exited one interstate and merged onto another. The woman seemed for all the world a New York Jew, but I knew one shouldn't suppose others' origins, and it somehow felt necessary to our site-visit esprit de corps to maintain a constant, if low-level, friendly chatter. "Are you from Dallas?" I wondered. "The TV show, *Dallas*," she responded. At least I could count on her to get my *Golden Girls* reference. I had been upgraded at the Four Seasons, and, indeed, I might well have been staying in the faux art deco Florida living room of Blanche, Dorothy, Sophia, and Rose. The floral prints, the rattan furniture, the bamboo fan lazily twirling in the arched ceiling; my villa's veranda opened onto a golf course. I related this to my colleagues over our pre-site-visit dinner, and Barbara not only recognized the parallel and recalled fondly the show—she was a lifelong Bea Arthur fan—but said team members *should* get upgraded on their first site visit as a kind of initiation into corporate travel.

Not so, Colonel Darren L., who didn't even bother to feign interest in my villa's architecture or decoration and instead rerouted our pre-site-visit dinner conversation to an NFL team, the Buffalo Bills. Over a steak the size of our rented Cadillac's hubcap, he lamented the Bills' lackluster season, one marked by external loss and internal struggle. Quarterback drama and intrigue, it seemed. "They benched Flutie," he said without making eye contact with either of his two dining companions; rather, he issued it more like a public declaration in the general direction of the restaurant's bar. Nonetheless, it was I who responded: "Doug Flutie?" My immediate recognition of an NFL quarterback and my ability to supply his first name was surely more surprising to me than to my site-visit companions, and no sooner had I spoken than the most specific reminisce sprang forth from the obscure part of my childhood memory palace that had been exposed to, although never that interested in, college football.

The carpeted lower floor of the split-level house I grew up in, a Saturday afternoon, the television on, but in rather decorative capacity, showing a college football game. A friend and I had made an impromptu fort from blankets, towels, and sheets, and the TV's antennae (we never had cable TV; air conditioning, either) formed one of our structure's unsteady ballasts. Said friend and I were playing on the floor doing something or other when one of us, I forget who, noticed the game clock had mere seconds on it. We both took note as the Boston College quarterback, a certain Doug Flutie, retreated behind his offensive line and sailed the ball indiscriminately toward the end zone, a maneuver of football desperation known as a Hail Mary. Such a pass is thrown in the closing moments of a game; one doesn't know the ball's precise destination—one only hopes one's own player takes hold of it for a touchdown. It could mean everything, it could just as well, and more likely, mean nothing, and, indeed, success might require a kind of divine intervention; perhaps it's worth noting that Boston College is a Catholic school. Miraculously, Flutie's Hail Mary was a game winner, one that enshrined him in college football history, launched him into the professional ranks, and, strangely, allotted him a place in my own idiosyncratic personal history.

By the time I had finished recounting my athletic tale, Darren L.'s attention had shifted. He became aware of me. And he, too, remembered that moment. "Flutie won the Heisman [Trophy] that year," he said wistfully of 1984. That pre-site-visit business dinner had become for me a kind of Hail Mary, too. But I wouldn't recognize the victory or even the stakes of the encounter until some weeks later—in the moment of my first business dinner what I did recognize was that Darren L., an Arthur Andersen Y2K site-visit expert, and I had formed a strange connection. He wasn't one to ask questions or really take note of others with any sense of intersubjective capacity, but my knowledge of mid-1980s college football trivia had been committed to Darren L.'s memory in a similarly random way to which Doug Flutie had been committed to mine.

68 | Fake Work

I make it sound like Dallas was a social engagement, which isn't entirely incorrect, and the next morning, as our gleaming Caddy pulled into the agency's parking lot, Darren L. did intimate that the aim of the meeting was more motivational than technical. "These site visits are a reminder to the agencies: time to get your butts in gear." Cindy had explained their necessity to me rather differently, but she, too, had stressed a relational component. "We want to encourage the agencies. But according to The Process, we can't do their Y2K documentation for them." After spending five months of doing little other than reading Excel spreadsheets of technological objects contained within the Conglomerate's various shops, I felt prepared. I had indeed been studying this particular agency's inventory rather obsessively: I knew the make and model of every piece of Y2K-vulnerable equipment they possessed—the obvious candidates like PCs, phones, printers, and fax machines, but more surreptitious ones, too: the HVAC system and the coffee maker, for example. "Anything with a clock is a risk," yet another of the New Hire Presentation slides had forewarned. As our team was escorted through various anodyne hallways and sterile antechambers into an equally characterless conference room, I scanned the environs for clocks or anything clocklike, but also for causes, for information, for seemingly benign objects that might warrant attention. I can't say I knew exactly what I was looking for, but I maintained my vigilance. And I recorded it in my Bildungsroman.

```
I guess it shouldn't surprise
me, but ad agencies have framed
advertisements adorning the walls,
like they were posters. This agency
```

> specializes in advertising for
> the medical profession and its
> pharmaceutical accomplices, so
> many of the framed posters are for
> prescription drugs. The framed ads
> in the women's room indicate they
> have the Tampax account.

My own private jottings indicate both an interest in the expanding terrain of my professional environment as well as an awareness of the banal character of the very industry we were all working so diligently to ensure would continue after January 1, 2000.

Since I uniquely occupied the overlapping position of woman and Quality Assurance Analyst, I would be taking notes, and I copied those into my Bildungsroman, too. As the site visit itself convened, and befitting his rank, Andersen Darren L. took immediate charge. The dramatis personae hardly require their own playbill, and here I list only those who spoke.

> Darren L.: Arthur Andersen manager,
> Y2K site-visit expert, Hertz Rental
> Rewards Colonel
>
> Leigh Claire: Quality Assurance
> Analyst, notetaker
>
> Dallas Roy: Y2K point person at
> ad agency, denim-clad, wearer of
> plumed cowboy hat

(He obviously wasn't named "Dallas" Roy, but he seemed to me so unbelievably and stereotypically Texan that I referred to him as such in my mind and in my manuscript.)

```
Darren L.:  All right, whadda we
got here?

Dallas Roy: You should have our
most recent inventory.

Darren L.: I haven't seen it.

Leigh Claire: I have a copy.

Darren L: Let me get a look at this
thing.

[long pause]

Darren L.: I'll tell you what I see
here, Roy.

Dallas Roy: Shoot.

Darren L.: Loose ends.

Dallas Roy: [looks down, softly
sighs]

Darren L.: I been on this project
```

about eleven months. Been to over ninety shops.

Dallas Roy: Man.

Darren L.: No one can say what's gonna happen, but it's gonna be tough. You gotta have things in order. Tight documentation. It's time to start thinking about worst-case scenarios.

Dallas Roy: I heard even houses weren't 100 percent safe.

Darren L.: Nothing's 100 percent safe. No such thing with Y2K. No one's got the expertise to fly this bird.

Dallas Roy: You nailed it, Darren. We're fallin' behind. We don't have the man-hours. We need help.

Darren L.: We got agencies from here to Timbuktu. Everyone needs something. This is what they get: quality assurance, oversight, site visits.

Our forty-five-minute site visit transpired in a conference room almost identical to the one in our New York office, with no agenda, no formal rituals, no nothing really, but said shop's inventory spreadsheets that I myself had printed out in our NYC office and transported with me. So eager had I been to grasp some material particular, to make sense where perhaps none was there to be made, that only once on the ground in Dallas did I realize that the point of the site visit was not to check the site but to document the check. It was a temporospatial expansion of The Process, but one still committed to a fundamentally textual understanding of the Y2K problem.

Darren L. was more garrulous than Guy, and without the latter's removed, scholarly quality. Business casual and folksy, a man of khakis, not of suits, of wrinkles, not of starch, he offered a different presentation of Arthur Andersen expertise. But his authority was just as absolute, his understanding of our historical moment just as concerned, and his solution just as textual: keep documenting. On my return to Midtown, Cindy q.a.'ed my meeting notes. She removed their carefully captured rhetorical flourishes so that by the time they were committed to the database, Darren L. did sound very much like Guy, and I sounded very much like her. She explained that The Process valued consistency over idiomatic accuracy, and she predicted that with more site visits I would find myself transliterating from corporate vernacular into Process Latin almost unconsciously.

It was usual to conclude a site visit with a decadent lunch, a way to relax after the meeting's intensity but also a platform to foster collegiality across the Conglomerate's often-fragmented global landscape. I felt slightly disappointed that my last moments in Dallas were spent at a corporate steak franchise near the airport's car rental return lot watching Darren L. sketch on a cocktail napkin the design for a new inground pool he was installing at his suburban home. At some point during our two days together, my intrigue at the psychic life of corporate power—here, an Andersen expert—had given way to a subtle, not fully realized, annoyance at his self-absorption. Of my site-visit time with Darren L., I finally, if dryly, commented in my Bildungsroman that `he ordered ribs and received an actual mammalian ribcage.` A vegetarian, I probably was discomfited by the whole lunchtime outing and made do with a salad or pasta, but of such an outcome I made no mention, nor do I have a memory.

Phase II:
Media and Mediations

My Putative Promotion

I never sought career advancement. So relieved was I to have a career—if you could call it that—that I had no desire to rearrange office affairs, to clamor, to draw untoward attention, or to fan the flames of a potential millennial Armageddon. The actual content of the working days of which my career was composed was lacking, sure. But that hardly lessened my satisfaction in having a career, in responding to post-collegiate entreaties regarding life's course with "I'm in quality assurance." Quiet maintenance was my approach. Fill out spreadsheets. Photocopy them. Participate in meetings in subdued form, as I had done in Dallas, all the while sharing, if modestly, the genuine excitement I felt to be included in such convocations. But capitalism expresses itself in unpredictable, often contradictory forms, a general tendency that I was to learn affects individual workers within a capitalist organization as surely as it does the system itself.

And Phase I: Inventory did not come to an end as an organic life process does. Rather, it was decidedly concluded so that Phase II: Media could begin in February 1999. The Y2K consultancy project that Arthur Andersen LLP had sold to the Conglomerate consisted of three phases, each one able to increase in intensity and to marshal more resources were the historical conjuncture to demand it. One wonders under what circumstances that conjuncture—with a possible ten months left before global technology might cease and with money to be made on the preparation for such a cessation—would not have demanded it. In any case, in that winter of 1999 the Conglomerate decided to expand its Y2K preparedness operations and brought more Andersen people into the office.

Phase II would initiate a "two-front war," in Guy's lexicon, against our shifting, chimerical adversary, Y2K, the possible techno-finale of modernity. The discrete processes begun under Phase I: Inventory would continue, as would everyone's adherence to The Process, but a flank would break off the main to confront any elusive Y2K problems lingering just below the surface, those found in the world's global media infrastructure, for example. One could feel a sense of anticipation in the office, and something seemed afoot on the twenty-fourth floor. In fact, the Andersen people had succeeded in getting a commission to conduct an audit of the mysterious Media Team, one of the few Y2K office groupings not under their administration. They would study the team intensely: examine its internal workings, read its emails, interview its team members, and then render an executive judgment on its very being. Guy had predicted the overall result in a phone conversation of which I'd only overheard one part when his door was serendipitously ajar and I was returning from retrieving yet another Diet Pepsi: "You can't do an audit and not find anything." Bloodsucking leeches indeed.

The Media Team was located directly behind my cubicle in an office, one to the left of Guy's, where two female analysts worked daily under the oversight of a male manager. All managers were men, so de facto, all women worked under male management. Still, since Leni's dramatic questioning of the Media Team's existential purpose, and the even more dramatic public repudiation of her for the inquiry, I had tried to take some notice of the Media Team's daily doings. They seemed to occupy themselves in a manner similar to that of other teams: printing spreadsheets, photocopying them, faxing them, putting them into binders, using a tab system to sort and alphabetize the binders' contents, and then, finally, alphabetizing the individual binders themselves.

Where the Media Team did distinguish itself was in its leadership. In an otherwise mostly white office, it was the one team run by a manager of color. The Conglomerate's Y2K office employed a few—like two—analysts of color. It had a Black database programmer and an Asian IT guy, but somehow nonwhite team members rarely percolated into upper management. Other than his race, however, the media manager had made little impression on me or, really, on most twenty-fourth-floor team members. His Media Team managerial duties demanded frequent and far-flung travel, and he was seldom in the office. Perhaps the only tangible bit of knowledge I had of his career was that he had somehow managed to board a plane to Brazil without having secured the necessary entrance visa. When he arrived in São Paulo, he was detained, denied passage, and put on a flight back to NYC. The business class cabin had no availability and he'd had to return in coach. It was a transnational snafu that hardly projected competence. He himself blamed the corporate travel agent, the gay and moody Carlos, and demanded his firing.

Instead, the Andersen axe fell on him. At the presentation of their audit to a coterie of Conglomerate higher echelon, a similarly sized coterie of Guy and Andersen top brass declared the Media Team was floundering. Here was a global media company, the Conglomerate, facing a Y2K threat to the very technology of media itself, and the team devoted to understanding media risks was asleep at the millennial wheel. The Andersen recommendation? The Conglomerate should fire its one Black manager, clear out any of his remaining loyalists on what came to be known as the old Media Team, bring more Andersen consultants into the office, and let them staff a new Media Team. Thermidor-like, the manager of color and his two underlings were summarily dismissed, and a novel Media Team order was constituted with the arrival of exactly one new Arthur Andersen consultant, Jennifer.

She was the Andersen person who had authored the Media Team audit, who'd executed the coup de grace, and it was she who now took the reins. Her first move was into the old Media Team's office; her second charge was to populate her team. The Conglomerate had agreed to Andersen management of the new Media Team, but not to Andersen rank and file staffing of it. That left Jennifer on the lupine prowl. She needed someone of Andersen quality but not Andersen price, someone familiar with The Process, someone who had been around the Midtown block and who had the battle scars to show it.

"Darren L. actually suggested you," Cindy said, after she'd asked me, for the first time since my hiring, if I had a moment and invited me into her office. Its window office looked down Fifty-Fourth Street, toward the famous Ziegfeld Theatre, and she made it her mission to keep the office abreast of afternoon preparations for red carpet events. She once claimed to have spotted Nicole Kidman getting out of a white limousine and, another time, she believed she'd identified Sarah Jessica Parker's dog walker. (`She's like Jimmy Stewart in Rear Window,` I joshed in my Bildungsroman, `waiting, watching, learning patterns.`) "Me?" I had to double-check, thinking it could it be a case of mistaken identity, like when a child first learns subject pronouns and, because they are addressed so often as "you," come to think "you" means "me." But, as if to stress she indeed meant me, Cindy qualified her statement.

"You impressed him in Dallas." Really? I did? On reflection, I suppose I had handled myself with a certain corporate savoir faire, and likely the Hail Mary conversation had differentiated me from the pack. What other prospective new Media Team member could recall a 1980s career-defining pass from the quarterback of Darren L.'s favorite football team? But I had hardly imagined I was auditioning for a new position. "You impressed me, too," Cindy continued. I'm not sure I had yet received a single Quality Assurance-related compliment, so to have two arrive in rapid fire was as pleasing as it was disorienting. Not that she was done. "I've just finished my review of your Dallas site-visit notes. We can't mention Timbuktu, for legal reasons, but otherwise. . ." She had more to say. Much more. But as she continued, her subject became less directed at my corporate past and more oriented toward my corporate future. "On the new Media Team, you'd actually be helping with Critical Management Considerations," she predicted. "Think of it as a promotion."

Those exact, conditional words I would later have some occasion to parse. Cindy was presenting an opportunity for corporate advance—that much was clear. But if it was one so sterling, why offer it to me? The office was brimming with eager notetakers and devoted quality assurers. What precisely had I done or, more worrisome, not done, to earn this managerial attention? And why couldn't Timbuktu be included in the official Dallas site-visit notes? The only possible explanation I could conjure was that the city had been renamed in a decolonizing wake, like

Mumbai for Bombay and Sri Lanka for Ceylon. None of this I could ask directly, of course. But nor could I shake the suspicion that I was being squeezed off the most respected team for a frankly unimpressive one. So I equivocated. On epistemological grounds. I rattled off a quick corporate listicle:
- I didn't know what the Media Team did, no one seemed to.
- Leni had been placed on a private shit list for even asking.
- The team manager had been denied entry to Brazil.
- On the stormy seas of the oncoming third millennium, the Media Team seemed rudderless and adrift.

As quickly as I offered a hesitation, Cindy answered it. So I changed tactics and pleaded loyalty to Quality Assurance. We were almost finished with our q.a. of the inventory database—we had located around 6,700 typos, many of which had been remediated and all of which had been documented as the result of our efforts. After such a collective accomplishment, it felt an odd time to forsake my team for another. The Dallas trip, too, had portended more good things for me on the QA Team. There had been some talk of me joining, in note-taking capacity, a site visit to a Los Angeles agency, whose focus was interactive interstate billboards.

In talking to Cindy, however, I realized that just as the offer to join the Media Team was to be *thought of* as a promotion, it was also to be *thought of* as a choice. We were having two parallel individual conversations more than we were responding to each other. Sitting in her boxy office, her veneer bookshelf full of proprietary binders, plaques, medals, and other official recognitions of her professional attributes, along with several unopened canisters of Play-Doh, she began a kind of free associative corporate ramble whose ultimate point was that an Arthur Andersen audit always augurs improvement and whose final, somewhat fantastic, hypothetical example was that of the United Nations, that body of global governance located only mere blocks from Arthur Andersen's New York City office. It was her dream, she said, for Arthur Andersen to audit the United Nations and to bring its members in line with The Process. "So many countries, so much overlap in roles and responsibilities, we could streamline all of that." She went on, rather like a modern-day Cecil Rhodes, the nineteenth-century British imperialist who famously looked into the evening sky and commented, "To think of these stars that you see overhead at night, these vast worlds which we can never reach. I would annex the planets if I could."[1] Cindy would audit them.

So now I would begin again, not as a Quality Assurance Analyst but as a Media Vendor Analyst. Changing teams meant moving locales and learning the ways of a new Cindy, namely the aforementioned Jennifer, whose ward I became and whose office I now shared. Perhaps the move from cubicle to office was part of my promotion, but Jennifer didn't understand it that way. "We're already behind. This will speed up communication." Nor had she realized that her auditor's report would become an epitaph on the grave of the old Media Team. Rather, she understood her original mission as: "Bang: audit. Bang: executive report. Bang: I'm outta here in two weeks." Her speech was rapid-fire and staccato, often condensed and always direct. The swiftness and unidirectionality of time itself demanded it, she claimed. To start tardy on a project whose nonnegotiable end date might well coincide with *the end*? The woman had no interest in pleasantries.

In contrast to Cindy's genuine enthusiasm for everything about management consulting (from the Play-Doh to The Process), Jennifer had a hardened corporate cynicism about her. I should have appreciated it, more redolent of my own disposition was her attitude, but I admit that I never entirely warmed to her presence, and I'm afraid that she felt similarly. She daily took calls from her interior decorator, the perfectly accented Yves, who, it seemed, was fifteen blocks away wandering around Upper East Side boutiques selecting upholstery patterns and end-table pairings. In those days before the instant exchange of smartphone images, Yves would engage in elaborate ekphrastic descriptions of this piece or that. Jennifer put these conversations on speakerphone so that she could continue typing with both hands, her manicured nails dancing above the keyboard with such intensity that often she had to ask Yves to repeat himself.

She overheard me, too, of course. (Although I very much doubt she was taking notes.) Ever-nosy Leni had learned that our Y2K office had a surreptitious toll-free number that, in the case of an advertising-oriented Y2K emergency, Conglomerate employees the world over could call to solicit expert advice: 1-800-Y2K-SAVE. But it was March 1999, and the specter of a time bomb 2000 detonation resonated as emergent more than an emergency for most of the world's advertisers. In the meantime, in those days before widespread cell phone adoption, when long-distance call charges, calling cards, and pay phones were inconvenient facts of relational life, team members in the know had begun giving out the office 800 number: friends in California and Canada, those who lived in Massachusetts (like my girlfriend), family (mine was in Virginia), anyone could chat with any team member toll-free. Indeed, if one could have elevated oneself to some panopticon-like vantage and surveyed the Y2K office in its entirety, at any given moment, one would have seen half of the office peering into spreadsheets and the other half on the phone. I now realized some not insignificant portion of them were engaged in free long-distance telephony.

As I narrate it now—somewhat distinct, it must be said, from how I narrated it then—my putative promotion to the Andersen-run new Media Team, somewhat ironically, initiated a kind of slow diminution to the end of my management consulting life. Perhaps fittingly, the best metaphor derives from athletics, although not from the team sport of football but from the individual pursuit of tennis, where, as an amateur player, I had found it was often easier to compete against a tougher opponent than a weaker one. The latter demands little and inspires less; the former, however, encourages concentration, solicits respect, summons her competitors to her own level; one knows one must be that good. That had been me on the Quality Assurance Team, playing above my level. Spreadsheet after spreadsheet, one line of meaningless inventory data after another, I persevered. Cindy's leadership and the esteem with which Quality Assurance was held on the Conglomerate's Y2K project required such a posture, and somehow, in response, I equaled the occasion. But things were to have a different contour on Jennifer's new Media Team, where a combination of indecision, indifference and pettiness verging on aggression, and a lack of professionalism (plenty of it mine) did not allow for expression of team members' best corporate selves. Equally notable is that the team's somewhat collective lack seems not to have affected the denouement of Phase II.

No corporation is an island, and to place its advertisements and solicitations the world over, the Conglomerate relied on the commercial assistance of media vendors, those who vend their companies' medial time and space. The objective of the Media Team was to inquire into the state of Y2K preparedness for the Conglomerate's top five thousand, give or take, most important global media-vending partners by mailing them a Y2K Preparedness Questionnaire. After all, were a certain media vendor with whom it had booked an advertisement to go black on 1/1/2000, where would that leave the Conglomerate? In a place of legal liability, if you asked Guy. Now imagine that every media vendor everywhere in the world went offline in concert—what would that do to advertising? We were about to find out. Or at least ask a few probing questions.

The new Media Team had inherited from the old Media Team a bulging, imposing binder of spreadsheets labeled "Media Vendors." The database programmers had constructed a media vendor database. A "data dump" would transfer the contents of the binder into the database, assign each media vendor an ID number, and then populate that entry's address field. We would utilize those addresses to mail each vendor the Preparedness Questionnaire. In fact, one of Jennifer's first tasks as new Media Team manager was to organize all this information into a PowerPoint slide.

New Media Team

-Media is Y2K mission critical

-Is designing Y2K Questionnaire

-Will be contacting Media Vendors

The New Hire/Executive Council Presentation—I had since realized it was really the only Y2K presentation that the Conglomerate possessed, one which was amended for whatever meeting the Conglomerate either hosted or attended in which it hoped to display its own Y2K preparedness—was retrofitted to include the Media Team's slide. Jennifer, likewise, had the slide rendered in poster board size and affixed it to a wall in our office, where its pabulum functioned as a kind of North Star of tasks. Bullet point three fell to me: "Will be contacting Media Vendors." It sounds as easy now as it was, on my part, naive then.

Because before any such event like mailing a questionnaire to an address transpired, a quality assurance check of every address in the media vendor database was required. Someone needed to identify the bugs and niggles, the oddities and infelicities, the doubles and deletions, that even the cleanest data always seems to include. That someone would be me. Thousands of entries to q.a., each with multiple lines of text and trailing series of numbers. The most fluorescent, crippling moments from the Quality Assurance Team would now be repeated. The database, the spreadsheets, the checking of the documents, the documenting of the checks. But worse. For a blonde QA twin I was no longer. Now I'd work alone, spiritually speaking, without the hesitant solidarity that I once found with other QA Team members at the photocopier. Yes, there was Jennifer, stationed some fourteen inches away from me in our eight-by-ten office. But we rarely spoke. She preferred to keep our communications written, she said, so that in the event of a lawsuit a record would exist. At least in our office we had a window. Not that it opened.

As media things developed, a difference did emerge, and on the path to Y2K-preparedness, the Media Team took a few shortcuts. Foremost, The Process required that the analyst who found errors was not the analyst who fixed them. Such a separation was Andersen's nod to what in business is called an "arm's length transaction." That distance of a metaphorical human limb forms a cardinal rule of accounting, valuation, exchange, all transactions, really, and it addresses a simple fact of our age: one can't just make things up or do as one pleases and call it capitalism. Rather, certain rules must be adhered to, a field of legitimacy must be established and cultivated; it must be collectively maintained and appreciated. The role of auditor is to ensure such a state of affairs. But not so here. If corners were being cut, it was the auditors wielding the proverbial scissors.

Because I located database errors. And then I amended them. The Quality of our Assurance had been lessened. We had our reasons, of course, foremost the swiftness of history but also the position left to us by the old Media Team, whose shaky foundation we had inherited. Jennifer had described it as: "A disgrace. Chaos was what it was." Then again, everyone has their reasons. The result was that not only did we lack a metaphorical arm's length distance between assessor and executor of deed but we didn't even have the length of my own bodily extremity. The same right hand, the same adjacent right arm, that moved the cursor from one database entry to the next—mine—was the one that completed the work of remedying the faulty entries.

I should qualify that these were not the kind of world-historical failures one associates with an impending global techno-calamity. These were more like address errors. Some countries don't have zip codes, they have postal codes; one had to be careful not to mislabel one as the other. That was one pitfall. Some jurisdictions place a country's name before the postal code, others after; yet another potential quagmire to which I had to attend. Addresses in Japanese characters had been transliterated into Roman script by the database, but sometimes errant punctuation marks were included in the result. Those too had to be spotted and removed. Misplaced commas, uncalled for and sometimes unintelligible abbreviations, mysteriously blank lines in an address entry, the expansive white of their digital nothingness glowed on my screen as a kind of subtle reminder of the emptiness of everything. On those longest and darkest of Media Team days, I wondered whether *the end* would really be so terrible.

In spite in my recalcitrance toward and resentment of working on a second-rate team—I tried to hide both; only my former team member can judge my success—and Jennifer's own unfriendly, if impressive, self-involvement, the Media Team continued "going forward," perhaps the single most uttered locution of historical motion at the Conglomerate. "Going forward" indicated progress, and it required collective effort. We were always "going forward." The phrase likewise bestowed a power on its speaker: to signal "going forward" was to claim a future being shaped—it was *that* forward to which we were all going. Of course, one could also use it in opposition, to chart a different future and to subtly signal a rerouting without a grand proclamation. "Going forward," your antagonist says, "we'll do X." "Going forward," you reply, "we'll do Y." One going forward to another.

While it was true that only after the completion of my quality assurance labor could the mailing of our Y2K Preparedness Questionnaire commence, it was also true that its mailing was an already compromised operation. It's a tricky risk proposition to mail unsolicited and legally implicating requests to corporate partners the world over, but in our case, Jennifer said that The Process demanded it. The Media Team would be sending around five thousand Y2K questionnaires, one to each address I had q.a.'ed, to the Conglomerate's most important media-vending providers, whether a radio station in London, a newspaper in Mexico City, or a television station in Tokyo, to ask what, precisely, they were doing to prepare for Y2K. But we knew very well that those five thousand media vendors wouldn't respond to our Y2K questionnaire because the Conglomerate itself didn't respond to the thousands of questionnaires it received from its own business partners asking basically the same question: What is the Conglomerate doing to prepare for Y2K? Jennifer explained that The Process wouldn't allow us to respond because of the legal vulnerability disclosing such information to another company created.

Such hopeless foresight spoke to an appreciable difference between Phase I's Kafkaesque routines and the rather Sisyphean elements of Phase II. Not his entomological *The Metamorphosis*, however, but his labyrinthine *The Trial*, is the Kafka that speaks to those first months of my corporate life—the childhood phase, perhaps, in which impenetrable codes and rules beget more of themselves. Where did they come from? Why are they here? Can they be outmaneuvered? One will never know. Mythical Sisyphus, however, understands everything, and that knowledge forms part of his punishment; it likewise resonates with the tone of Phase II, my corporate adolescence. Sisyphus is condemned for eternity to roll a boulder up an incline, and no sooner does he complete his task then it rolls downhill and he must begin again. The penal conditions that shaped Phase II of my corporate life wouldn't endure for all of time, but it seemed very likely they would last the next ten months.

That kind of team rationale was only one of the reasons that work on the Media Team managed to be more dispiriting than that on the QA Team. Please, give me Modernist estrangement over Existentialist dread any day of the working week. There were others, though. Many team members were trotting the globe conducting Y2K site visits of the kind I had done in Dallas, and the twenty-fourth floor took on a transient, desolate quality. The speckled white dropped ceiling seemed to sag under the weight of the HVAC infrastructure it was meant to occlude. The Diet Pepsi began to leave a sour aftertaste. Guy decamped to Asia for two weeks to provide auxiliary support for a series of Y2K regional meetings. Cindy headed for Vancouver to instruct the Conglomerate's Pacific Rim shops in the ways of The Process. Darren L., a corporate peripatetic, circulated from one business class lounge to another—alerting Conglomerate shops the world over that the end was closer than it seemed. Even the usually sedentary Justin took a premillennial working tour of Paris, Brussels, and London with a group of analysts in tow.

It fell to Leni to reveal what I should have already known. That mine had been a fake promotion. She did so while we were eating lunch at one of those expansive by-the-pound corporate salad bars that proliferate in Midtown delis and that, no matter how disparate their menu or varied their clientele, somehow always manage to include Mongolian barbequed beef, stuffed tilapia filets, and baked macaroni and cheese—its orange top layer so crusty one could skate on it. She spoke, and I immediately recognized her truth. Perhaps I had been moved laterally, perhaps even that was too optimistic of an assessment. Some clues were obvious. I hadn't received a raise, for example. Others, more subtle. Quality Assurance Analyst has a certain corporate gravitas to it, but what would Media Vendor Analyst mean on my resume, if I did want to leverage my Conglomerate time into a future Fortune 500 life? She observed my simmering angst and provided a new German term to add to my Bildungsroman: *weltschmerz,* or world-weariness. It's a philosophical condition that often accompanies one's adult-aged realization of the full disrepair of modern life, a kind of mix of ennui and loss. Leni said I was suffering from it. She advised me to open an E*Trade account and to orient my portfolio toward biotech. She staked out a position in Amgen and had, within some months, doubled her money. I followed her advice, and it did prove a salve, albeit a temporary one.

If The Process did offer me any salvation that potentially apocalyptic spring of 1999, it was located in its self-metabolizing structure. All activities done in its name needed to be documented, and such documentation takes time. It likewise imposes on time a certain flexibility. The more of The Process the Conglomerate purchased, the more documentation of it there would need to be and the more time it would take. Even as the apocalypse hovered on the horizon, always one day closer than the previous day, the work of this Media Vendor Analyst remained the same. Notwithstanding Jennifer's call to maintain a posture of "going forward," some days I'd spend hours examining a single database entry. I might well have been trying to divine truths from an Aramaic scroll—but it did allow for the elapse of time—if that were a benefit. I could no longer tell. Weeks and then months passed in a fugue whose only rationale was "documentation." When I wasn't documenting for the Conglomerate, I was taking my own notes for my Bildungsroman.

I suppose I should be impressed with myself that I kept writing under such life-limiting conditions. Yet the prose I produced during that cruel season lacks any sense of ethnographic depth or richness. Instead, it offers scene after scene of dialogue. Laconic exchanges, mostly about deli lunch orders, between Jennifer and me. The Media Team office abutted Guy's, and when both doors were open and the whirl of the printer and beeps of the fax machine were momentarily suspended, I might hear a whisper of his corporate sotto voce. "Another rat fleeing a sinking ship," he once said, to someone, about something. Pre- and post-meeting chatter at Wednesday's conference room assembly. Snippets from the General Meeting itself. Justin: "We ain't getting any younger. Neither is Y2K"; and one random bit of the General's political philosophy: "Most women won't say they're feminists because they don't want to be seen as lesbians." Details of Leni's fascinating unfolding biography, the Fraus and Frauleins, the *Torten* and *Lederhosen*, her family stripped of the aristocratic "von" in their surname when Austria abolished its nobility.

A few lines from that early iteration have borne well the passage of time—almost all dramatic uses of the word "fuck" and other profanities amidst otherwise banal office banter. But for the page-after-page of prosaic documentation I generated, not much of value may be retrieved. Things actually got to the point, it seemed, that not only did my fake promotion to the new Media Team short-circuit whatever potential my corporate life may have possessed, but it also began to depress my budding second career as a writer.

A Total Bitch and an Absolute Fraud

It often happens to those attuned to life's strange antimonies and antagonisms that a roadblock becomes a new path. An end cedes into a beginning. An obstacle reappears as an opportunity. Sadly, in my early twenties, I wasn't one of those people so attuned. If I encountered a metaphorical brick wall, it was my instinct to add to its fortifications. I rued the misfortune of my new team and my new team leader, Jennifer. That inner employment-oriented turmoil, I can now report, might have been experienced differently. My Bildungsroman evidences this possibility, and the reams of notes from my Media Team time that never made it into my manuscript's many drafts demonstrate that I did find Jennifer captivating. Yes, she repelled me. But she intrigued me as well. She still does. And the reason I could never succeed in my many attempts to write a section about Jennifer is that, as the Buddhist nun Pema Chödrön instructs, life's difficulties do not truly depart until they have taught us what we need to know. What I didn't understand then but have since realized is that it was the placement of Jennifer into my daily world that compelled me to face with sober senses the real condition of my working life, as well those of my relations with my corporate kind.

Still, it's one thing to retrospect and quite another to endure. And part of my general Media Team malaise, both its spiritual and textual expressions, I do attribute to Jennifer. The woman affected a presence both distant and demanding. She prickled easily. And there we were, stationed mere inches from each other for eight hours a day with the weight of the media vendor world straining our already computer-hunched shoulders. She rarely spoke. To me, that is. To her decorator, her mechanic, her country club's reception desk (its golf pro shop, mainly), her jeweler, her travel agent, her husband, mother, and brother, to them she rattled on ceaselessly. There was the time her heat pump zonked out during those transitional, nonetheless often chilly, days that span late winter to early spring. The technician said it would take two days before he could attend to it. He might well have been a firehouse refusing to attend to a five-alarm conflagration at a children's hospital, and Jennifer's extended network sprang into action to demand, and achieve, redress.

Her daily-task- and social-engagement-concerned speech often disoriented and rendered me into a kind of dissociative state to the point where I couldn't focus on the work of comparing a media vendor address in the binder to a media vendor in the database. Once I hinted that she might curtail the chatter. Even finding an instant when she wasn't on the phone to ask for this basic office pleasantry proved challenging. I waited for a propitious moment, one between calls. It occurred sometime between her reserving a tee time for her husband and a (seeming) confirmation of a lunch date with her mother and aunt. Jennifer's response arrived without correction, concern, or eye contact. "So move back to your cubicle." The gall. The tone. Were we on the same team, or not?

Lacking in the appropriate corporate and class armature, bored and defenseless, I became subsumed into Jennifer's atmosphere—an uninvited interloper, a visiting ethnographer not only of a management consultancy but of the psychic interior of a native consultant. I would peer into another world whenever I needed to vanish from my own, composed, as it was, of a binder of media vendors' addresses. But was it Jennifer herself or the asymmetrical distribution of power and wealth in our relationship that jaded, disturbed, and, it must be said, entranced me so? This question seems important to answer, and my early attempts, which constituted far too much of that initial draft of my Bildungsroman, were both truncated and misdirected, concerned as they were with Jennifer's rather ostentatious lifestyle and her obliviousness thereof.

```
Jennifer's Mercedes is back in
the shop—caliper problems. That's
only one of today's Media Team
revelations. The other? Her husband
has a penchant for difficult-
to-obtain dog breeds, and they
imported a Rhodesian Ridgeback
from South Africa. But they worry
they got a dud. The beast fears
precipitation. Over the weekend's
snow shower, it refused to leave
the house and shat in the foyer,
the very one Yves had interior
decorated. Now they are considering
legal action (against the breeder,
```

```
not Yves). I know this because she
speaks on the phone with impunity,
as if I'm not there. And I listen
with a different kind of impunity,
as though I am.
```

In trying to capture her pettiness, I inadvertently captured my own. It's a common enough creative falter, and there are few writerly tasks as challenging as maintaining a reader's interest and sympathy during an extended rant, a diatribe, really, against a middling, modest sparring partner. So she and her family watched the Golf Channel and thought corporate law an intellectual pursuit—was that really reason enough to condemn them?

Let me try again. Jennifer was "a total bitch." But those aren't my words. I did not claim any such thing in my original manuscript. Aware as I was then and remain now of the misogynistic implications of that ironically canine word, I rarely use it. I didn't describe Cindy as such because such a statement bore no truth. I even thought about not employing the term now, in *Fake Work*, because, frankly, the atmosphere around Arthur Andersen and the Conglomerate was hostile enough to women. But part of this version of my book, of its now-retrospective element, is to bring in new sources, mostly Marx-oriented, but some not, whose absence caused the first version of "Bildungsroman: A Year in My Life" to stall and to be ultimately abandoned in the early aughts; July 2004, to be exact. One aspect of revision must include offering team members the same benefit of hindsight I have offered myself, and more than any other team member, it is Jennifer who now reappears on her own terms—"bitch" is one of them.

Yes, my dour Media Team colleague who didn't speak to me for months on end and once pretended not to recognize me at an overpriced, European-inflected Midtown grocery, became, in her second corporate act, unexpectedly loquacious. Perhaps she had no choice. After Arthur Andersen LLP—at the time, the world's second-biggest and probably most legendary corporate auditor and consultancy—exploded like a cheap firecracker, Jennifer's employment there ended, of course. The firm was court ordered to cease its operations, its limited liability partnership was dissolved, and all its employees with their proprietary knowledge and best practices were released hither and yon to roam the mean streets of Midtown. It's easy enough to abstract to the general facts of Andersen's sudden and surreal demise. The multiple accounting frauds brought to light; eighty thousand–plus employees terminated; billions of dollars in capital dramatically vanished; the Big Five corporate accounting firms, suddenly, and still, the Big Four. But what of the intimate particulars? Had Yves finished decorating Jennifer's suburban mansion? What of her children's college funds? Plans for a summer house? A winter one? Jennifer's own words tell the tale. "I created an at-home business when I lost my job due to an industry scandal with all of my kids under the age of 5!"* She really did exclaim this, somewhat off-tone in my opinion.

Nor does she, in this interview, explore the precise nature of the "industry scandal"—she doesn't even identify the industry! It's not really an interview. It's more of a public-facing, staged, Socratic self-introspection. Except that it's not very introspec-

---

* From the "about us" feature on Jennifer's business's website. The business, what we might call the empowerment of female entrepreneurs facing trying moments in their personal life, is co-owned.

tive. Rather, she conducts her own back-and-forth, between Jennifer and Jennifer, with an eye toward public relations. Why did she start her new business? What does she offer? Are you a potential client? Let us see. Tasked with reconstructing her professional life anew in a new millennium, Jennifer became a social media influencer, one who counsels businesswomen, one who attempts to help others avoid her corporate fate, and one who has a prolific and self-disclosing online presence.

I understand why she omitted her previous career as an Arthur Andersen auditor. Her former firm's demise was an unsavory business, front-page fodder, and not just in the business press. If corporate accountancy ever had its moment in the sun, then the late '90s and early aughts were it. Sadly, for those employed, any such illumination was of auditors who knew full well that the figures didn't add up, but who were making too much money to turn off the spigot of accounting and consulting fees. Not a day passed in the latter days of the dot-com era, it seemed, when some audit was revealed as off or when some correction to a financial statement wasn't being issued. Even before the Enron debacle, Arthur Andersen had suffered a few instances in which it had been caught in flagrante delicto. Like their late 1990s turn at the Waste Management Inc. wheel when they flagged $1.7 billion worth of improperly presented profits and losses, only to allow themselves to be bribed into not reporting any of it. One wonders if the resulting $7 million Andersen had to pony up in fines from the Securities and Exchange Commission not only failed to act as a "moral hazard," to use the corporate law vernacular, but in fact egged them on.

Because with their Enron auditing and consulting, Andersen took it to the next level. If there were a company to risk it all for, it was Enron, once described by the *New York Times* as "a new-economy company, a thinking-outside-the-box, paradigm-shifting, market-making company . . . [one] ranked as the most innovative company in America four years in a row, as judged by envious corporate peers in the annual *Fortune* magazine poll."[1] Enron was an energy company that didn't so much produce or distribute energy as it did buy and sell positions on the price of energy stocks—derivatives. And Arthur Andersen guided them. The auditing side of Arthur Andersen collected fees for certifying Enron's public financial statements, while its consulting side collected fees for advising Enron on best practices. But the financial statements contained fictional elements, and the "best practices" were those of rearranging, scuttling, and obscuring. Massage the losses. Underestimate the debts. Report loans received as profits made. Off-load liabilities into subsidiaries. Hide who owns them. Claim profits before any are made in anticipation of them someday arriving (that one wasn't even illegal!). Do it all to keep the stock price high; keep doing it to nudge the stock price higher. It's not that plenty of publicly traded companies don't do this. And it's not that plenty of corporate auditors and accountants don't sign off on it. But Arthur Andersen was different. They got caught. Not with one pathbreaking, new-economy company, but with two.

In fact, the pair of scandalous bankruptcies that ended the dot-com bubble once and for all were those of Enron and WorldCom, a new-economy telecom. Both had Andersen as their auditors, and for both it was Andersen's seal of approval that allowed these companies to float their soon-to-be-worthless stocks. At WorldCom, it allowed billions of dollars of crash-inducing debt to be tidily tucked away. And it had been certifying inflated earnings reports for Enron, whose imaginatively construed frauds included hollow subsidiary operations named for Star Wars figures and a $100 million loan from a Canadian bank that was reported as a profit.

When Andersen had its license suspended for their repeated negligence, they went into crisis mode. They had to act. It was like a cartoon version of a corporate caper—quick! If we destroy the document trail, no one will ever know. Once the suicides and prison sentences began at Enron upper management, that's when Andersen broke out the ol' paper shredder. Then they got slammed with criminal obstruction of justice in addition to their loss of licensure. The Enron failure, itself the largest corporate bankruptcy in US history, generated the eminently sensible question "On whose watch did this all transpire?" The answer: Arthur Andersen's. The *Wall Street Journal* published a series of postmortems to the idea of greatness and legacy in corporate accountancy—"An Andersen Old-Timer Recalls When Prestige Was Bottom Line"—announced one rather sententious headline.[2] Other questions, in the form of *New York Times'* headlines, were more critical. "Enron's Collapse: The Auditors; Who's Keeping the Accountants Accountable?" Then, some days later, another Andersen-focused investigation titled "Enron's Collapse: The System; Web of Safeguards Failed as Enron Fell." And another: "Enron's Collapse: The Accountants; Watching the Firms That Watch the Books."[3]

For Jennifer, I surmise, but certainly for me, the nothing of Y2K when it came and went, followed by the near-simultaneous collapse of Arthur Andersen, then of the stock market (more on that, in a sec), then of the World Trade Center, left a sense of, really? Y2K, a joke. Arthur Andersen, a fraud. The economy, a fantasy. The World Trade Center, a military target. I was almost glad that that famous picture of the Loch Ness Monster, the one of its long neck and perfectly shaped head jutting out of the inky Scottish lagoon, had been revealed as a fake in 1994, because if a reevaluation of Nessie, too, had been forced on me in the early 2000s, I think I would have breached my limit of idols felled and darlings killed.

One picks up the pieces and tries to make sense where one can. As it all crumbled in 2002, I went backward, as it were, and attempted to understand then-present economic events through historical study. As a PhD student in the early aughts, I began regular travel into the archival world of the 1980s economy, a decade of financial scandals big and small, individual and systemic. Economic things, I was forced to conclude, fall apart with the surety of other things. Jennifer, perhaps unsurprisingly, took a different approach. She went forward and attempted to render the nothing of her destroyed Andersen experience into a something, a new career in a new millennium. One might say that Jennifer became an independent businesswoman, and I became someone who collects odd tales about business, including hers.

Jennifer ping-ponged around various consultancies, before transforming into an entrepreneur of herself, one who peddles different genres of businesswoman-centric self-care to her audience. To do so, she presents stories and images, she gives advice and sometimes even quizzes, she invites her followers into her life to witness not only her triumphs but her sorrows. Her brand: how to be a hard-nosed but successful female in a cutthroat world, one who cares for herself, her children, and her relationships; how to be resilient; how to overcome obstacles; how to insist, and mean it, that every day is a new day; how to persevere; and how, when life drops four hundred pounds of lemons at your suburban door, to dust off the old citrus reamer and not only make lemonade but open a lemonade stand—perhaps, even, franchise it. "I like having my own money," she explained of her own fiscal acumen in the same prospectus in which she mentioned an "industry scandal" "and [I'm] not afraid to work for it."

There's more. She included interviews with several of her associates to provide, I imagine, a candid look at the woman behind the selfie. Here are several choice lines on what initial reactions to Jennifer yielded in terms of character assessment:

"what a bitch";
"so standoffish";
"my first impression of [her] was: a total bitch."

I see their point. Jennifer had a coldness, a simultaneous lack of curiosity and empathy. Of course, these women eventually overcame the jolt of their primary judgments; she included them as testimonials to her own self-presentation, after all. Yet Jennifer and I never moved past that unfriendly distance of first impressions. I can't be sure of her assessment of me, probably "suspected homosexual." She ran our team, of two, like a medieval suzerain, and had I died in a metaphorical famine, she would have replaced me with another potato-picking peasant. More worrisome still, had the whole corporate house of Y2K cards collapsed on the Media Team, and had Jennifer and I been left alone to face the millennial music in a court of law, it would have been every man for himself, of that I am regrettably sure. And now I was violating The Process's rules and norms. A few times I couldn't verify a media vendor's address, so I just deleted the whole entry. Once, it may have been on the Ides of March, a combination of annoyance, exhaustion, and eye strain led me to realize full well that a certain address contained mistakes—a Canadian postal code always has letters in addition to numbers; this one didn't. It had been corrupted—but I certified it and moved on, nonetheless.

Under Jennifer's weary tutelage, I had become a case study in bad practices. The very reason The Process demanded its unique division of labor, at least two sets of eyes on each database entry, was so that opportunistic team members didn't go AWOL in a fit of delirium or frustration. Think of it as the management consulting equivalent to the famous separation of roles during nuclear preparedness exercises: one cold warrior holds the key and the other has the code—only together can they launch a nuclear strike.

And Jennifer, the Media Team leader, did she notice my procedural waywardness? Regarding some things, I'm sure. She had asked the IT crew to make work I did in the media vendor database visible to her, in real time, from her own computer's desktop. She could monitor my keystrokes and surveil my punctuation amendments when she saw fit. Sitting Sistine Chapel–like, with hand-of-God-touching-Adam closeness, we could have brushed fingertips across her desk had we each extended our arms. Instead, she'd send me a frosty, officious email if she noticed a media vendor address error. Fine. But did she care? Certainly, she wanted to impress Guy and the other Andersen people. But about the possible end of the world? I would be surprised if she ever gave it a passing thought. She conducted herself professionally, but I sensed a lack of spiritual commitment of the kind that motivated the other Andersen people and that leads many of them, even to this day, to maintain an Andersen alumni association under their famous heteronormative "Think Straight, Talk Straight" banner. They reminisce about audits conducted and proprietary trainings attended. They remain saddened and remorseful about their still-cherished firm's rather embarrassing exit from the business world. A glass case of Andersen memorabilia on permanent display at the University of Illinois Chicago actually includes the two imposing wooden doors to the first Arthur Andersen office.[4]

With the benefit of time, I've come to realize that the bitchy elements of Jennifer's character interest me less than does her class composition, of which bitchiness formed only the most basic introduction, a sort of handshake. Jennifer typified a different element of the professional managerial set—she was out for herself, not her kind. She presented as an Arthur Andersen consultant but also as a free agent. Gone was the cause; dismissed was the belief in something bigger; "Think Straight, Talk Straight," was for her a phrase to rehearse rather than an ethos by which to live. And Jennifer's understanding of economic totality began and ended with Jennifer. In one of our few conversations, she related that her husband would likely make partner at his boutique investment bank. Then things would be changing, she said. But only for her. "With this whole thing," she meant the economy, "it's the wives who benefit."

Or not.

Because not only was her employer, Arthur Andersen LLP, a fraud, but so, it turns out, was her husband. Jennifer did endure a forced humbling, but its source was not that her entire corporate world and professional identity was revealed to be fake.

Speaking to a podcast about her business venture, she recounts the moment she realized that her life was not what she thought. There she sat, alone in her car, on Mother's Day. An unknown number rang her cell. Already something felt urgent and unusual about the call. She usually didn't get cell service in the location. But the phone rang. She had a policy (don't we all?) of not answering unknown numbers, but something—perhaps a not fully conscious awareness that things were off—prompted her to do so. Then she heard a woman's voice: "Is this Jennifer Y., and are you married to Mr. Y?" "Yes," Jennifer said, with some trepidation. "Well, I'm engaged to be married to him," the voice responded, "and I have been for over a year."

Even the most hardened and cynical of corporate actors can surprise, and I think Jennifer would probably agree with Karl Marx that humans do make their own history, even if, it's true, they do so not under conditions of their own choosing. Because what did Jennifer say when given the news that her most intimate relationship was as corrupt as an Andersen audit? Did she call the woman who had cuckqueaned her a family-wrecker or a dime-store slut? Did she doubt this woman's veracity or threaten her? Not at all. In fact, what Jennifer reports is as graceful a response as I, probably as anyone, can imagine. "And I said, 'Thank you for calling me. You saved my life.'"

It is in trying to make sense of our post-Andersen lives that Jennifer's and my narratives, once so disparate, an intimacy forced by an awkward office seating arrangement of all things, meaningfully converge. We both emerged into the nascent third millennium Y2K-unscathed and, surprisingly, unemployed. Jennifer, by corporate faux pas, and me by choice. We shared the experience of safeguarding media from a Y2K meltdown, only to have the company that had done the safeguarding itself meltdown. Then we both underwent, I think it's fair to say, a Copernican revolution, a forced reevaluation of the most cherished and orienting of values. Jennifer became an entrepreneur of herself, and I became a student of Marxism.

A Tepid Marxist and a Bubble Popped

So how did I become a Marxist ethnographer of large corporate organizations, and only a moderately successfully one at that? This is my first real published ethnography, and it's as much a self-ethnography as an outward-facing one. It's also a bit anachronistic, historically speaking. I had hoped to publish it twenty-five years ago, coincident, you know, with the event in question. I could offer some excuses for the delay, but I certainly can't place any significant portion of the blame on Jennifer. Historical trends more deterministic than a management consultant with girl-boss energy and a semi-tragic historical arc have brought me here. Yet the Andersen people undoubtedly nudged me leftward, politically and intellectually. And the first book I wrote and actually published—it was about postmodern literature and finance, release date 2014, from Oxford University Press—bore the imprint of my corporate years as surely as this one does. Maybe the more appropriate investigation, then, is not why I become a Marxist when I did, but what took me so long and what had Y2K to do with it.

Because I never set out to study organizations or political economy. But as much as I had longed for a life of corporate knowledge work—with its stability, salaried recognition, hoped-for distinction and inclusion, simultaneously—the spoils I had to that point received had failed to generate the associated affects I presumed would accompany them. I had wanted to give capitalism a try, to intercept it on my own terms so that I could evaluate it with some amount of dispassion. Not that I hadn't been warned, both emotionally and intellectually, about the qualities of my economic adversary. In college, the campus anarchists, disorganized though they were, had become friendly acquaintances of mine and had pamphleted the dorm hallways for years with calls to walk away from the system and from what their Kinko's-copied posters claimed were its various racist, classist, genocidal, and imperialist logics.

But I walked toward it. I wanted to sell out, and I believed I had something available for purchase. "Maybe you'll have a few hobbies, but that's it," predicted, in a lecture, one of my political theory professors on the implications of understanding Marx's vision of an alienated working life. The scene he sketched was a despairing one in which so much energy and emotion is forked over to the employer that all one really has left for oneself is collecting oddments or practicing as an amateur sports commentator—the kind who broadcasts to one's family from one's own couch. Honestly, it sounded OK to me. It was one of many arguments I misinterpreted that semester—that his was a criticism and not an invitation.

He might have presented the matter differently. And he was well positioned to do so. To teach, he wore jeans, a white Oxford cloth shirt, and a thin black tie, its Double Windsor dangling some two inches below his collar's top button in a declaration of studied but carefree casualness. He inflected his lectures with appropriately placed expletives. His students, I among them, were ready to be moved. But he never pushed, really. Of course, every interpreter has their own Marx, but his was a rather peculiar one. He conjured the philosophical spirit of a progressive professional liberal who might have voted for Bill Clinton and sent his offspring to private school while simultaneously leveling a totalizing critique against the progressive professional liberalism and privatization that Clinton introduced. The 1990s were famously a decade of irony, and that, my very first Marx, was imbued with a strange ironic nihilism. Your work will exhaust you, and you'll still do it because what else is there to do. Your wedding will be boring and bourgeois, and you'll still have one because individual sexual love offers what little redemption you're likely to find. Your children will be as entitled as you are, and you'll try to please them nonetheless. Let bushy, bearded Karl and clean-shaven me detail for you a guide to the travails inherent in your privilege, he seemed to offer.

I understand that the seemingly always-autumnal foothills of Western Massachusetts, from the lectern of a private college, no less, was not the most opportune place to call for an overthrow of the capitalist state. But we might have read more than *The Communist Manifesto*, a poorly excerpted version at that? Not to mention the fact that the theatrical and declarative anachronism of that famous text's opening lines—"A specter is haunting Europe, the specter of communism"—often confuses college students, especially those like me who had been to Europe and seen nothing of the sort. Rather, while in France, I'd made a pilgrimage to Jim Morrison's lovingly desecrated Paris grave and delighted in watching leash-trained cats parade through the Luxembourg Gardens. The very genre of a manifesto encourages bold claims, of course, and Marx's *Communist* iteration doesn't disappoint. "Society as a whole is more and more splitting up into two great hostile camps, into two great classes directly facing each other—Bourgeoisie and Proletariat." That, too, stretched my comprehension. One would think such a grand chasm easily spotted. Instead, a majority of the US working class had cast their lot with bourgeois millionaire moralist Ronald Reagan—my vote for Michael Dukakis was the sole one in the 1984 straw poll that Mrs. Brubaker had run in her otherwise apolitical third-grade classroom. Nor did Marx's understanding of domestic matters unveil to me any obscured truths. "The bourgeoisie has torn away from the family its sentimental veil, and has reduced the family relation to a mere money relation." I saw no such evidence of that transactional logic in my family, unless we count the fact that my parents paid me to mow our modest lawn.

I maintain that while in college, I should have been presented a different, less thematic and more economic selection of Marx's oeuvre. I attempt to do this with my students. But, in all truth, certain key points likely would have bypassed me still. Ironically, one of them being that an individual learns the laws of capitalism "as a man learns the law of gravity when his house collapses on him."[1] Two retorts here, both equal in importance. First, it was only after working with Andersen and at the Conglomerate that I would be able to understand Marx in any meaningful, analytic sense. And second, the house did collapse.

House as in the "new economy," the dot-com economy, the internet bubble, of which a company like Enron was both an emblem and a part. From what I could glean in 1998, this new economy was similar to the previous economy, but different.

True, some of the basic, what we might call "old economy," rules still applied—wage labor, for example. One continued to offer one's time to an employer and one got a predetermined sum in return. Hierarchies between workers and managers remained the order of the day, with the former assuredly subjugated to the latter. Money, too, seemed to retain its centuries-long importance. Not that the new aspects lacked charm, either: office-hosted buffet-style spreads that included artisanal potato chips and a variety of kombuchas; a lack of walls; Aeron chairs, able to bob, swivel, and adjust in at least forty possible combinations; an allowance for sweatpants and sneakers in the business casual dress code; the hope of a stock windfall.

I, for one, bought it. Sign me up. In fact, those new-economy companies had passed on hiring me. I did land one interview at an internet start-up called Juno, named for the Roman goddess of matrimony and childbirth; also terribly vindictive, she dispatched two snakes to kill the baby Hercules. Sadly, my knowledge of ancient mythology got me nowhere near the new economy, and instead, I was employed by a decades-old advertising company with office furniture to match that midcentury origin. But the zeitgeist permeated nonetheless, as infectious at Andersen and the Conglomerate as in emerging silicon alleys and valleys of the late 1990s.

The truth was that during the intensity of those premillennial days, so concerned had everyone been to ward off Y2K, a fake crisis, that several real ones had been left to fester. But there they dwelled, and by the late '90s/early aughts, American economic infrastructure was inviting of any number of surface-to-essence-to-nothing metaphors. As the stock market edged higher, the precipice edged closer, and the slightest nudge or mildest breeze was sure to be a disaster. That proto-disaster might have arrived in the form of Y2K—not for nothing was there a thumbtacked article in our twenty-fourth-floor kitchenette whose headline broadcast "economist predicts Y2K recession"—but alas, in the words of Gertrude Stein, there was no there there.[2] The there was rather everywhere else: in the technology-oriented NASDAQ stock index, up 800 percent and then down 740 percent in a matter of several years, from 1998 to 2001. Companies' securities filings had begun to include certain fictitious elements, accounting reporting standards were adjusted to produce stock-worthy values, flimsy strictures of economic decorum were made flimsier; Enron was the model.

It was hard not to see the frankly surreal economic environment in which I had been immersed. At its height I had, for example, attended a party given by a fledging e-firm that promised to deliver still-dripping hot fudge sundaes via moped to densely populated urban areas. When they realized theirs was a fatally hobbled business plan, they threw a party at their headquarters in Chelsea, NYC. My invite came via a prospecting friend who'd stumbled into a job writing ad copy for the firm— her starting salary was $100,000 a year, but she never wrote anything. During the party, cater waiters adorned in hot fudge motifs doled out extra-sweet and boozy cocktails. At one point the whole soirée moved to another building floor, whose construction hadn't been finished—windows nothing more than gaping holes; aluminum studs stood where walls might have been or perhaps still might be; a giant plastic tarp functioned as a kind of barrier to the elements, billowing and bowing out to expose Tenth Avenue below as the February wind whipped through the mass of drunken revelers. When said friend commented, "I half expect to see my boss in a toga, eating grapes on a roman couch surrounded by a harem," it felt utterly sensible. The end was nigh.

Then there lurked the stubborn phantom of a question of what had any of it been for and where would it take me? My education, I mean. Its philosophical component, in particular. (Although it was hard to deduce that a vocational training left one in better stead; the Andersen engineers and business grads were populating and photocopying the same spreadsheets.) As my cohort left its liberal arts crèche and began to navigate transactional life, the idea was less that philosophy would be a Grand Inquisitor and more that it would offer a kind of companionship, like an emotional support animal. Exposure to it would percolate rarefied thoughts, and these would accompany one on one's disenchanting voyage through adulthood, perhaps whisper a kind word before death, not necessarily to ease one's suffering but to contextualize it. Philosophy would not, however, provide economic context while the thinker was alive.

A differently educated observer might have noted the structural indications of gravity's force before any actual house razing. The slowly diminishing interest rates and their profusion of ever-cheaper money brought forth to banks and corporate coffers by the end of the 1990s. The 1996 Telecommunications Act—an opening up of an entire industry to new prospecting, new alliances, and new investments, a commercial internet among them. There were hiccups, too—leveraged ones like the Long-Term Capital Management crisis and its Fed-organized bailout. As Conglomerate team members sat dutifully photocopying our spreadsheets in 1999, the Glass Steagall Act, introduced during the Great Depression, was being reconfigured, removing barriers between consumer and investment banking and teeing up a crisis that would emerge fully formed in the 2007–08 global credit crash.

I didn't see it coming. Any of it. That much should be obvious.

But what did the Marxists augur? That seems the more relevant question—especially since they won me over and, in a way, saved this book from the dustbin of history. A retrospective perusal of their late-second-millennial broadsides and political economic analyses confirms that they harbored suspicions. While much of the business press and academic world was celebrating the novelty of what had been baptized the new economy, an economy of e-commerce, buyable and sellable on E*Trade, boundless and buoyant, late 1990s and early aughts Marxist onlookers saw a darkening horizon.

Writing in a periodical whose sedate title *Monthly Review* might falsely give the impression of a retirement-home activity guide or a Unitarian church newsletter, they foresaw a global economy wracked by declension and depression. "A notable slowdown has also taken place alongside a major leap in technology, the so-called New Economy," they wrote. Not that they ignored the basic facts. They acknowledged, for example, that the infrastructure of the new economy was indeed new, but wondered: besides the newness, what of it? "Advances in information technology such as computers and the Internet—for all their impacts on office work, inventory management, etc.—have not yet provided the major stimulus that capitalism requires to maintain high growth rates."[3]

How different their analyses appeared from the editorial pages of the *Wall Street Journal* or from mainstream economists, some of whom were predicting an even more stratospheric stock market than the one we already had. One did so in the ambitiously titled book *Dow 36,000*, which they assured investors was within reach. (It would take the Dow Jones stock index twenty-four more years to reach that mark.) Others were encouraging people to read *The Millionaire Next Door* (paperbacks of which predominated at the Conglomerate; Cindy had a dog-eared copy on her bookshelf), a popular guide to personal economics that suggested that coupon cutting and mindful checkbook balancing had rendered an untold number of Americans millionaires, that they were everywhere, next door, even, hiding in plain sight, and that with thrift, enough readers could join them.

And yet the Marxists had begun to diagnose a "long downturn."[4] In the flashiness of e-wealth, e-business, e-work, they saw a terminally ill patient, capitalism itself, who summons one last bout of delirious, manic energy before keeling over and emitting a final death croak. In other words, for the Marxists, something was amiss. Indeed, as they called it, twentieth-century capitalism had spawned a few good decades, the so-called and already-mentioned postwar Golden Age. But thereafter, it had lurched from bubble to bubble, crisis to crisis, crash to crash, bailout to bailout. And the more this particular bubble, the dot-com bubble, the new-economy bubble, took hold, in daily discourse, in private imaginations, with the resounding popularity of the 1990s hit gameshow *Who Wants to Be a Millionaire?*, the more Marxian doom assumed seemingly fantastic dimensions. Gazing into the new economy, most economic observers glimpsed an El Dorado. The Marxists saw a swamp.

Had it occurred to me to read their work, had I even known it existed while a Media Team member, I'm quite sure I would have joined their camp—the contrarian in me wouldn't have had it any other way. It was that same unanalyzed kernel of proclivity toward opposition that had brought me to the Conglomerate in the first place. But, my private tempests excluded, let us give economic credit where such credit is due. The Marxists nailed it. The "so-called new economy" they positioned as somewhere between a Ponzi scheme and house of cards; its flimsy façade will crumble—they insisted—as surely as did the seventeenth-century Dutch tulip bubble, it just might take a little longer. Not much, it turned out. Tulip-mania lasted from 1634 to 1637; e-mania is dated 1995–2000.

Marxists have foreseen other historical flops, too, some incredibly specific. In *The Eighteenth Brumaire of Louis Bonaparte*, Karl Marx himself predicted the felling of a public sculpture, one that honored French wartime victory at Austerlitz. "If the imperial mantle should, in the end, fall upon the shoulders of Louis Bonaparte," he wrote of France's then-ruler, "the iron statue of Napoleon will crash from the top of the Vendôme column."[5] It happened, exactly that way, nineteen years later. In 1871, France was seized by communal fervor, and the Vendôme column, an awkward phallus of a monument to imperialism situated in the middle of a Paris traffic circle with a full body cast of Napoleon resting, cherry-like, on top, was toppled by communard revolutionaries.

Other Marxist prognostications have been a bit more spacious and urged followers to understand similar capitalist construction projects as fallen in theory regardless of their posture in physical reality. "We begin to recognize the monuments of the bourgeoisie as ruins, even before they have crumbled," advised Walter Benjamin. And if one can't subscribe to that act of imaginative disruption, that same theorist offers a way to conceive of continuity: "That things just go on is the catastrophe."[6] For Marxists, the crisis is always and everywhere. Yesterday. Today. Tomorrow. A hundred years ago. Another hundred from now. They see it in themselves. They see it others. If a society collapses, it's a historical failure; if it doesn't, it's a failure still. If history changes course, it's for the worse. If it maintains its path, it's just as bad. "History puts its worst foot forward," quipped another one.[7]

At a certain point, it does get a bit tedious and overwrought. I now suspect that my ongoing philosophical tussles with the legacy of Marx played some small part in the delayed publication of this book, at one point almost extinguishing it for good. They don't really have space for humor, personal reflection, or the waxing and waning of emotional cathexes that accompany any theoretical exploration. Their insistent negativity, their almost personal invective directed at the passage of time and most of its contents has, for me, over the course of a Marx-inspired intellectual trajectory, been both seductive and off-putting. Seductive at first. Off-putting as the years accumulate. One well-regarded, indeed quite brilliant and creative, Marxist theoretician I know dismissed the Atlantic, from shore to shore, as a "bullshit ocean." He compared it to its stately relative, the Pacific, as what a large body of water should be, as that to which the Atlantic aspired but could never equal in scope, grandeur, variation of wave and color, undulous landscape both above and below (how did he know?) the surface.

But that doesn't mean they are wrong, about economic history or, indeed, in this peculiar case about the Atlantic—it *is* cold and grey. I've gone on the record numerous times insisting that Maine's rocky, mosquito-ridden coastline is overrated. Nor does it mean I didn't find Marxist despair endearing. Because when I did, finally, join their moody tendency, I felt at home, comfortable in a way I never had experienced during my Conglomerate days. Cindy, about whom I did ultimately find many things to appreciate, never became a comrade.

There we sat in the midst of an economic bubble, the dot-com crescendo, which wasn't recognized as a bubble but rather as a genuinely new era, the titular head of "the new economy." Of course, the end of any bubble is ever present—that's what makes it a bubble—it's just not acknowledged. The reverse situation held sway in the Conglomerate's Y2K office, where the end of everything was acknowledged, constantly even—it just wasn't there. In those waning days of financial print culture, team members would excise Y2K-oriented articles from newspapers and magazines and thumbtack them to the office's cork bulletin board. Recessions, war, social collapse, no specter seemed too grizzly to consider: "Let's stop pretending that Y2K isn't a major threat to our way of life," Mr. Yardeni says. "This year the American economy is a supertanker, but next year it is going to be Titanic America."[8]

The funny thing, or one of them? For all their naysaying, their doom and gloom, when, everywhere, they perceived the end of the capitalist world, in Y2K, the Marxists saw only "a technical glitch."

> The new century and new millennium were supposed to symbolize that all of this had been left behind and that we could look forward to a new era of infinite progress . . . which would usher in a gentler, kinder, virtual capitalism. The main worry was a technical glitch known

as Y2K. Would computers across the world malfunction on January 1, 2000?[9]

Computers didn't fail, but almost everything else economic did. And then there was the personal level. To be a barnacle on the floating corpse of capital. Was that the most I could hope for from a professional life? It was a future about which I anxiously equivocated whether to affix myself. Perhaps I did so with slightly more awareness of the tides and currents than those around me, but little benefit accrued from my Weltschmerz. The marine metaphors that began to populate my Bildungsroman, meanwhile, derived from the world map that Jennifer had attached to our wall, opposite the poster board Media Team slide, to remind us of the extensive span of the Conglomerate and, correspondingly, the depth of its Y2K vulnerabilities.

My attention increasingly drifted toward the oceanic, advertising agency-less, regions of the world perhaps to match my interior sense of feeling unmoored. In one particularly pained and embarrassingly colonialist section of my Bildungsroman, I find that I included notes for a trip to Mauritania's stark coast, a place whose imagined dramatic emptiness seemed the only thing to which I could relate. There, without the infrastructure of Midtown, minus team members and lacking for soft drinks, even, in a situation so bleak and, for me, contextless, I'd be forced to confront myself and make some decisions about life. If the world survived Y2K, what would the third millennium hold for me?

The Process could reproduce itself textually forever and so, seemingly, could I. We worked toward different ends, of course. Shortly after the apocalypse, the ashes still probably smoldering, when all team members were sitting on those stiff, pew-like benches in court, on trial, and the Conglomerate needed to mount a defense, The Process would be trotted out as evidence. Armored trucks would arrive at our fabled New Jersey document warehouse, where endless reams of Cindy-collated documents were stored, all unimpeachable originals. They would bear witness to the reality of our mimetic office, where no deed was not premeditated before, documented during, or stored after, all ready for presentation. Were the integrity of a certain deed or decision, an action or a reaction, questioned by the prosecution, an archive so multifaceted and voluminous would descend on them that even wading through it would form its own defense. The very specter of the Conglomerate's paper monument might be enough to pressure its antagonist to settle out of court—in fact that was the goal. Process documentation formed a bulwark against litigation.

And my Bildungsroman, where was it destined? A surprise star witness at trial? Such courtroom dramas don't really exist, it turns out. Both plaintiff and defendant must turn over their evidence to the opposing side during discovery before a trial begins. Even so, in a court of law, my unfinished tome might not have proved helpful to the Conglomerate. Would it have been damning, "*This* is who they had assuring quality?" Or exculpatory, "At least she had an interest in corporate documentation." In fact, only Leni and my girlfriend even knew of its existence. I wondered if Jennifer suspected that I was writing a book. Perhaps she noticed the rhythms and pace of my typing, which certainly had little in common with the spreadsheet-oriented finger movements of an Arthur Andersen consultant; rather, they resonated with someone writing paragraphs, and many of them.

Strangely, however, her typing was like that, too. In our months of intimate office dwelling, I never understood what occupied her days other than her household management, even as I can assert that the intensity of her keystrokes, their rapidity, and the cold gaze of her monkish concentration, all led me to believe I wasn't the only suspicious member of the new Media Team.

My Joke of a Promotion

Even to this day, it remains difficult to quantify precisely how much of our twenty-fourth-floor office occupants' daily doings were totally fake. It's harder still to really get into the deep psychic reaches of various team members' minds to solicit their opinions. Now or then. Did Justin know Y2K had all the makings of a nothingburger? Did Jennifer suspect that Arthur Andersen had strayed from its founding values? And Guy? He must have had some awareness of something. The best available question today seems, if they had known, would they have cared? Here I feel more comfortable proffering that, no, they would not have. Not about the status of fraudulent Andersen, not about the fate of Y2K, not even about the condition of global advertising. Few people were concerned about climate change in 1999, and team members would not have been either. Their careers they were attached to. They believed in firms, if not their firm, then the idea of a firm itself, and what the firm was doing, they believed in. It's like when historians finally got into the secret Soviet archives only to find that behind closed doors, upper apparatchiks spoke about the same things, and in the same ways, they did in their public pronouncements—they really were believers. True, too, it turns out, for corporate middle management.

By April 1999, the Conglomerate's Y2K office welcomed that sense of earthly renewal that spring often brings. I had finished q.a.-ing about 4,859 or so media vendor addresses—so what if I skipped a few? Jennifer had provided the oversight; she had also hired a landscape architect to design her home's grounds. Guy gave the go-ahead, and we initiated The Mailing of the Questionnaire. The team used FedEx, of course, to have a record of each mailing, for documentation purposes. We were all too aware that in the event of a Y2K-spurred global media outage, the paper trail our team was generating could well prove crucial and exculpatory evidence. Because if a client, let's say Chevrolet, had contracted the Conglomerate to run an advertisement in Chile, and if on 1/1/2000 Chile had plunged into a hunting-and-gathering-like prelapsarian state and the advertisement did not run, it would fall to the Conglomerate to demonstrate that it had acted responsibly in a fiduciary sense when it had accepted the booking and that it had tried its best, again in a fiduciary sense, to place and execute Chevrolet's advert, as well as to be aware of any complicating factors. Thus we had a questionnaire bound for *El Mecurio,* Chile's Pinochet-supporting newspaper of record. What would we learn from *El Mecurio*? Likely nothing, but that wasn't the point. We tried. And we documented our trials. An epistolary musical chairs of Y2K questionnaires thus began; each day some were sent by the Conglomerate to its partners; each day some were received by the Conglomerate from its partners; almost never was there a day when any were answered.

Yet as Y2K-preparedness offices the nation over seemed suspended in kind of informational entropy—no Y2K knowledge could be ascertained or offered, for legal reasons; yet firms had to attempt to ascertain it, for legal reasons—my own Media Team's situation strangely improved. Either through kindness or cunning, resourcefulness or ruse, Jennifer successfully argued to the all-male managerial set that her position and mine were properly analytic in design and that sending and receiving FedEx envelopes was below our collective paygrade. We were approved to hire a temp, a sullen character named Rick, who was trying to break into the slowly consolidating world of trade publishing and who took up residence in my former cubicle. To the extent that there was anything material to be done, like printing an address label, affixing an envelope, or ordering a FedEx pickup, Rick did it. He then documented his doings. I checked his documentation. Jennifer provided the oversight to my check, and Guy sat, as always, atop our hierarchy of managerial needs.

Otherwise blank office days were punctuated by small moments of extracurricular pleasure. In a bid to keep their workforce healthy, the Conglomerate offered team members a gratis membership at a chichi Midtown gym, which I began to frequent during lunch hours so long they might have been construed as truancy. A treadmill run, a schvitz and long shower—these are all truly the mood boosters they are reputed to be. I noted but was not disturbed by the fact that I was the only woman in the locker room with pubic hair. One day, semi-naked at the bank of hairdryers and complimentary skin care products, a ghost of my past appeared, a certain Florida-raised Lauren, who I knew from tennis camp. Years later, there we were. Both in Midtown Manhattan, both "in advertising," no less. Our recognition was equal and simultaneous. We'd spent two long southern summers chasing errant felted balls and doing speed drills in the Virginia sun. By that point in my corporate life, I had accepted that my own position was likely fake, and I was beginning to suspect the entire Y2K affair had a certain fraudulence about it, too.

But this was too much to communicate over a damp and slightly awkward locker-room embrace. We had around four minutes or so to catch up on the last ten years of life. Did I come out to her? Tell her of my parents' divorce or of my subsequent substitution of recreational drugs for tennis as a sixteen-year-old? Confide in her about my aunt's untimely death from Lou Gehrig's disease, or relate the central argument of my senior thesis on Hannah Arendt's use of Kant's *Third Critique* in her theory of political judgment? In fact, I only said, "I'm a Media Vendor Analyst at the Conglomerate." She could hardly believe it. She was an analyst, too, at a different advertising conglomerate. Somehow, via overpriced private higher education, we'd both managed to transition from an upper-middle-class recreational sport to corporate knowledge work.

Such encounters only made me appreciate Leni that much more. I anticipated what had become our regular post-workout deli lunches like a child does a story hour. Over our Styrofoam plates and disposable sporks, when the Sturm und Drang of the Conglomerate, the Media Team, the apocalypse, receded, Leni held forth. Her father had cut a cruel figure. Not that he didn't have his own tribulations. He'd been shot on the Eastern Front and more or less crawled back to Vienna. A skilled marksman who excelled in deer hunting, the goal of his postwar life was to bear a son. But several marriages later, he had only Leni, whose own goal in life it became was to flee him. Her first out, she had promised herself, she would take.

The exit came in the form of an American park ranger, in Vienna to study German forest management, who could hardly believe his luck. He'd landed a fallen Austrian aristocrat, one whose family had once owned some impressive percentage of the country's woods. Charmed by a scene of wall-mounted, fourteen-point buck heads and afternoon Sacher torte, he had insisted on asking for Leni's hand in marriage the old-fashioned way, after receiving the permission of her father during a manly sylvan wander. The patriarch responded, "Fine, take her," but warned his future son-in-law against the union; "A man should do better." Then our lunch hour was over, the shrapnel of our conversation left at the deli, and we were back on the twenty-fourth floor superintending various prophylactics against the end of the world.

With Jennifer at the helm and Rick a sturdy oarsman, I, through no doing of my own, assumed that awkward position of middle management. It seemed to be my station in life to sit on West Fifty-Fourth Street until my job or the world ended. One of the two would necessarily happen on or about January 1, 2000. What more had to be done? Any office action could be described and, according to The Process, it had to be. The switchback between action and description really knew no limits, except for those imposed by capital itself—basically, a certain percentage of workers had to remain alive and our labor had to be temporally demarcated. With their smoking, red-meat consumption, and sedentary habits, there was genuine reason to wonder about the first of these requirements being met at the managerial level. Would they all make it? But what the managers' lifestyle choices lacked, the time-bound nature of Y2K itself compensated for. To be was to document being, and The Process would remain operative until the very event around which it was structured had been traversed, namely, the clock striking (or not, as the case may have been) 12:00 a.m. on January 1, 2000.

These externalities limned our office. They provided certain allowances and required still other sacrifices. Traditionally, advertising agencies adopt a summer schedule and close on Fridays. So regular has been this seasonal work reduction for so long that it's often considered an industry perk, and team members indeed had been known to select the profession based on it. But as New York's humidity seeped into May's calendar to herald summer's arrival, Justin announced during one of Wednesday's General Meetings that given our office's extraordinary historical circumstances (he appealed to the law of force majeure), no such dispensation would be offered. Even though team members understood the logic of his decision—the doomsday clock was ticking—office morale took a swift and precipitous dive.

In response, Justin, impromptu, organized an all-office fieldtrip to the Six Flags amusement park in New Jersey on one summer Friday to compensate for all summer Fridays. Team members were invited to enjoy liberally the concession area and to test their height and speed thresholds on a variety of architecturally imposing rides; a tour bus chartered from Midtown meant no one would have to navigate the PATH train. Rick and the office temps were included in a show of team generosity. The scene one imagined was rather surreal. Guy, in his pressed suit and wingtips, playing mini golf while sipping a Diet Fanta; Jennifer's angular face feigning joy, but not well, as the multistoried roller coaster on which she rode lurched over some sheer-faced vertical drop; Justin, I could see as boisterous and tipsy, actually enjoying himself, beer in one hand, cigarette in another, a Yankees cap on his head—he'd selected the destination, after all; Cindy, too, would have fun, taking notes and distributing drink tickets.

When I cited my history of mild acrophobia as reason to opt out of the event, Jennifer asked me if I were "trying to destroy [my] career?" Her direct question surprised me, and not only because we rarely spoke to each other. Rather, I felt unnerved that her understanding might be shared by other team members. Indeed, Justin soon interpreted the actions of those few team members who had declined his invitation to be assumed as hostile, a kind of friendly fire, and we were told we would be expected at the office that day to sit alone in what amounted to a corporate time-out. Leni played it better. She called in sick with food poisoning on the morning of the field trip, and, after expressing both abdominal discomfort and emotional regret, she spent her day at home.

I was not rehearsing for a premature exit, however. Nor did I harbor a repressed, psychoanalytic-style wish to be fired. But nor, still, could I imagine the Conglomerate or Arthur Andersen as my life's calling. It was one thing to pout and fret when the work deadened and demanded, but quite another to do so when, essentially, I just had to sit there, on low-level alert, for a predicted apocalypse some months away. Was I as smart as the Andersen people? I think so, probably. But I can't say it helped matters. They may not have had a critique, but they did have a place in the order of things. Like them, I had chosen to be there. Unlike them, my selection of career began a kind of subtle but nagging psychic disorganization in me.

My Bildungsroman became more introspective, a solipsistic turn from which, in its first, millennial instantiation, circa 1999, it never really recovered. Sometimes the instruction to "write what you know" isn't the best advice, particularly for a novice sitting in a Midtown skyscraper.

> I never once considered that just as these types wouldn't recruit me, I wouldn't want to be employed by them. That maybe their screening processes work and I should have been deselected. That a weeding-out would have been better. For me. But now I'm here, I have been hired. I wanted to see something different and nonacademic and personally profitable and, in that sense, I got what I came for.

The odd thing remains that the more I lost my way, the more, somehow, I wrote. My Bildungsroman became a strange, Babel-like counter-archive, one which I could get into but not out of. The Process and my book-in-progress formed an equal part of my prison house of language. To make sense of the language of the first, I elaborated and, I hoped, analyzed in the second. I intended my elucubrations as critique, as that which grabs hold of some Archimedean point, somewhere, and uses it as a conceptual lever to pull author and vantage point above the fray and render an otherwise obscured truth available for all.

Unfortunately, for me and any prospective readers, that didn't happen. Far from Archimedes, I stumbled on Jared Diamond, an evolutionary biologist turned best-selling pop-science author. Any number of Marxists would have been better, but they didn't appear on the display table at the Rockefeller Center Barnes and Noble, the only bookstore I really frequented during my corporate days. Diamond did. That first full draft of my

Bildungsroman quotes his *Guns, Germs, and Steel: The Fates of Human Societies*, whose subtitle seemed to capture the problem of our collective future as the new millennium bore down. In his exploration of what makes humanity tick, Diamond writes that technology "exemplifies what is termed an autocatalytic process . . . one that speeds up at a rate increase with time because the process catalyzes itself."[1] His understanding of technology misrecognizes its structure—it's a form of collective labor, not a teleology—but as a metaphor for capital, Diamond provides some proximal accuracy.

Still, my own problem resulted less from the fact that I needed a metaphor and more from the fact that I was unaware that a metaphor was what I had. Y2K presented a metaphor for "this whole thing," in Jennifer's words. Without that basic understanding to undergird my prose, my critique fell as flat as the joke I had made that working within the ambit of The Process was like the passage of time in *The Magic Mountain*. ("Is that at the one in Florida or California?" Cindy had asked.) My Bildungsroman spews a litany of examples of corporate irregularities but fails to display an understanding of the norm from which such instances deviated.

```
A batch of Y2K questionnaires was
returned as undeliverable—not
that it's so different from the
usual "no response." Is this how
companies are put together? I find
it incredible. These are the things
that organize global commerce?
Run governments? Fly planes? My
```

`second-grade soccer team was more carefully recruited and managed.`

I was appalled at what I considered the sheer wastefulness of the entire enterprise, with no realization of the fact that, at this level of corporate composition, money cannot be lost, only spent, because circulation itself is part of the point.

It's also part of the point of what the foregoing Marxists meant when they said things had begun to sputter, and then stall, economically around the time of my birth. The internet be damned: "a notable slowdown," they claimed, had taken root. Capitalist economies, since the mid-1970s, had been beset by "a long downturn," they insisted. As they saw it, there wasn't much for capitalists to do but push the status quo down the line, take a cut, and hope to get on the right side of a financial bubble. A bubble grows rapidly, and with pleasing geographical symmetry, but the more any bubble—financial, soap, plastic, what have you—expands, the more pressure points are created, the puncture of any of which may induce collapse. We weren't there yet. But we were close.

One hundred thousand dollars for a pointless questionnaire mailing; $1 million (at least) for a world's worth of useless Y2K site visits, and we weren't even done; the Conglomerate's actual headquarters were located six blocks away, on Madison Avenue, and a trusty fleet of black town cars maintained their readiness to shuttle the all-male managerial team to and from our Sixth Avenue millennial outpost; $4 million for the fraudulent Andersen Y2K project, not that a nonfraudulent one would have differed so substantially in structure or cost. And not that it mattered. Like a shark, capital needs to be in motion, or it dies. Unlike a shark, capital is already moribund.

That was the point at which I truly needed a certain nineteenth-century German critic whose gothic metaphors reveal that "capital is dead labor, which, vampire-like, lives only by sucking living labor, and lives the more, the more labor it sucks."[2] But without him, I focused on myself, and, god knows, I was being bled dry. Conceptually, I mean. It's like I was attempting to judge the size of the Empire State Building without looking up, to type while wearing mittens. I highlighted symptoms as if they were causes, with no recognition that causes were things bigger and beyond my office window, out of whose view, if I pushed my face to the glass and craned my neck, a vestige of Central Park became visible.

Then, right when it seemed that no event could break through the stranglehold of The Process, that nothing would change, that even the end of the world could be absorbed, recorded, and archived in a climate-controlled New Jersey data warehouse, that the poststructuralists really were right, that the world is a boundless, infinite text, something actually happened. Jennifer left. Her parting became a kind of Memorial Day 1999 gift to me, and her interior decoration of our office with a world map, somewhat fittingly, constituted Jennifer's last real Media Team decision. Team members often arrived and departed on the twenty-fourth floor without notice; people quit and were fired; team members from various Conglomerate outposts were suddenly amongst us, and just as suddenly gone. Jennifer would now join the latter's ranks. She would become part-time at the Conglomerate and would begin to work with other Andersen clients. "Going forward" she said, she would "roll on" and "roll off" the Media Team as The Process required. Six weeks of overseeing questionnaire mailings and receiving boilerplate responses that no response could be given for legal reasons had convinced all interested parties that the Media Team was progressing smoothly toward doomsday, and a coalition of managers had determined her continual presence redundant. I never saw Jennifer again. Her final phone call in our shared office was to book an annual maintenance appointment at a Midtown jeweler for her watch. Rick would be kept in abeyance in his cubicle in the unlikely event of an uptick in Y2K questionnaire response volume.

I would, for all practical purposes—not that there were any—become the manager of this diminutive team. "I guess that makes you our Media Director," Justin joked of me at our weekly General Meeting, announcing Jennifer's departure under the Cindy-prepared agenda's bullet point: "Personnel Change in Media Team." A ruffle of modest chuckling ensued around the conference room table. It's a commanding title at any advertising agency, Media Director, one usually not achieved through jest and one that includes managerial responsibilities beyond an office temp and what I suspected was his clip-on tie. Nonetheless, I went with it, going so far as to venture into Justin's lair to inquire if my new position came with a raise, unlike the initial conceptual "think of it as a promotion" transfer that brought me to the Media Team in the first place. Our conversation had the potential to feel awkward and embarrassing, for both of us, I think. Instead, with a look of some surprise at my earnestness, he offered me ten grand more a year and issued me a warning about the responsibilities that came with a pseudo-managerial role: "If even a single [Conglomerate] agency experiences so much as one Y2K glitch, my career and yours and everyone else's around here is fucked. That's what I say when people ask, 'How's it going?'"

While I don't have a record of the exact words used in my response, I'm quite sure that I offered a gesture of appreciation for my new post as well as one of concern for the fate of the modern world. In my most narcissistic fantasies of grandiosity—a few months under Jennifer's middling thralldom had chipped away at their foundation to the point that only their shadows remained—I had never considered a Media Directorship among the possibilities of my corporate life. But embrace it I did. I had new business cards made; I purchased a lighter, more appropriate to summer, suit, its color a kind of hopeful beige. The spiritual pendulum of corporate labor's alienation had begun to swing in the opposite direction, and not a moment too soon, frankly.

Yet if Justin's warning sounded not quite so dramatic to me at its moment of utterance, it's probably because I'd begun to suspect that much as the Andersen people exaggerated the need for their services—could anyone else be trusted to make a photocopy or sort a three-ring binder alphabetically?—Justin inflated the risk that doomsday posed to the Conglomerate. If the Conglomerate did indeed make it to the other side of January 1, 2000, who would be more feted than the man who had delivered it from near certain ruin? Meanwhile, the more Andersen charged for the project, the bigger Justin's budget needed to be, and the more he became a manager of Big Budgets. For Guy, the reverse of the scene prevailed: an Andersen partnership was right there, ripe for the taking. The Andersen people often whispered about this, the "p-word" they called it, when Guy was out of earshot: Would it come this week? Next month? Ever? Its impending bestowal almost functioned as a kitchenette parlor game—one that I was not above enjoying as a spectator. Guy had to show he could reel in the big clients, charge them for everything, turn The Process into an inescapable stricture: bill the client to get in, bill 'em more to get out. If it took spending a summer Friday at Six Flags or sacrificing a little lung capacity from secondhand exposure in the managerial smoking closet—then so be it.

With six months left before a possible techno-Armageddon, everyone had a part to play. Mine was now to oversee Y2K preparedness for global media operations at the Conglomerate, one of the biggest goddamned communications companies in the world. As a result of the 2007–08 global financial crisis, really the culmination of our earlier exploration of capitalist setbacks, the old Winston Churchill–inspired, Rahm Emanuel–adopted, saw "never let a serious crisis go to waste," has made something of a comeback. A similar logic applies to an unserious crisis, too—perhaps even more so. With a serious crisis, one can imagine well the stakes; one understands the scope; thus, an urgency may be motivated and actions come forthwith. But with an unserious crisis, how does one find one's coordinates? Where does one apply oneself, and to what end? How are the various strands of disbelief suspended and reconciled?

Cindy received the news of my fake promotion wearily. I was her quondam Quality Assurance adjutant, and now I had become an equal, if ersatz, team leader. Would I now share her stature around the office? Not really, as it happened. Sometimes Leni insisted I pay for our deli lunches—"Well, you *are* the Media Director." Would I now attend proprietary conclaves with Guy? In fact, he only addressed me by name once, and it was the wrong one. I had been retrieving a Diet Pepsi from the kitchenette when he entered it and headed for the mini fridge. He was the only male team member who preferred his Pepsi products low-cal, and in a gesture of team cohesion, I intercepted him and handed him a can. "Appreciate it, Leigh Ann," he nodded. Before I could say, "Of course," much less correct his nomenclature, he and his soft drink had vanished into the fluorescent haze.

Something was rotten in the corporate state of Denmark, and while the decay could have found a sturdier example than me, the trajectory of my career did index a strange, if not surreal, culture of work at the Conglomerate. I'd been there long enough to know that recruiting new employees was a chance operation. Managing them, too, was handled with a certain indifference. Ascending to the ranks of the hierarchy I had presumed would have more of a meritocratic element, but my own fictitious promotion to a managerial post belied that hunch.

Much of this pained Cindy, who understood corporate capitalism and the management thereof as the pinnacle of the human sciences and who embraced its truths in a manner usually found in religious devotees or political partisans. She indeed viewed much of what transpired daily at the Conglomerate as a kind of profanity. Cutting corners on the Media Team; flamboyantly defying The Process during the General Meeting's "What's Good? What Needs Improving?" exercise; not staffing properly Andersen teams fully with Andersen people; and, now, promoting me. The Media Director had no clothes. As if all of this weren't painful enough, its realization further compounded her suffering, as it induced in her a kind of dysphoria, namely, that the same worldview that oriented her being *also* commanded that one respect a client and believe in a client's ability to flourish under The Process. I had then encountered few people with such a sense of devotion to anything, and my Bildungsroman contains several clumsy reaches for a language in which to comprehend Cindy's fealty. The woman embraces the corporate world with an absolute *joie de vivre*. Structures that seem to me dumbing and daunting, like audits, are felt by Cindy to be genuine aesthetic experiences, I noted. Continually amazed by her knowledge of The Process, I suggested that she is either prescient or omnipotent or probably both. I'm relieved to see a moment of self-reflection, too: What is it about my strange attraction to/revulsion from Cindy as a corporate experience? I asked in my text but could not answer.

I think I can now, a perhaps necessary aspect of this self-referential, narrative, and often auto-ethnography. Had I devoted all life's energies to accomplishing what Cindy had, I would have failed. Even if I started over, now, knowing what I do, I'd likely still fall short. I actually blind-guessed on the math portion of the Graduate Record Exam. Her sterling high school record. Her Ivy League admission. She'd excelled there, too. In a field overwhelmingly dominated de facto and de jure by men, she'd been a feminine, and maybe even feminist, standout, more by example than intention, but still. Then the Andersen post. Of course she'd risen the consulting ranks, and done so expeditiously. She had never, it seemed, had an off day—at least not when it mattered. Did she ever say, "Fuck it"? Did she ever think it?

In our many months together, I only once heard her utter an unkind sentiment about her firm, Arthur Andersen LLP. This while I was keeping an actual book of every thought, statement, action, or reaction I found untoward at my own firm, the Conglomerate, and hers, too, by association. Cindy had journeyed to Vancouver to oversee several Y2K site visits. An Andersen person, though, as she was undertaking a Conglomerate trip, the Conglomerate would pay, and she'd use the Conglomerate's corporate travel services—thankfully, no visa was required. She returned even more buoyant than usual. Confident not only that the Conglomerate's Vancouver shops could survive a Y2K hit but that with the frequent-flier miles she had accrued, she could book a trip to the Cayman Islands with her college sorority sisters. Amidst her otherwise good cheer, however, she related that when traveling for Andersen, on its dime, consultants were forced to relinquish any accrued frequent-flier miles, hotel loyalty points, and car rental rewards.

Offensive as the news was, it was less what she said than how she said it. Her tone forlorn and almost embarrassed for her employer, there was a tinge of moral outrage, too. What did the Andersen partners need with their employees' frequent-flier miles? No sooner had she revealed this information than she began to disavow it, in it a show of genuine loyalty. The situation wasn't ideal, she acknowledged, but who was she to question the prerogatives of the Arthur Andersen partners in what amounted to a kind of "live by the sword, die by the sword" moment. All she could hope, she said, was that the policy might be reconsidered. Hers was a remonstration hardly necessary. If given the chance, even then, before I had the concepts I needed to thoroughly understand the whole of my experience, I would have condemned the partners outright as thieves and miscreants—and not necessarily because of their mileage-usurping policy. Rather, I enjoy condemning people who occupy positions of what I consider excessive authority.

When the crash arrived and everything collapsed—Andersen, the dot-coms, the stock market, the World Trade Center—two years had already passed since I'd worked at the Conglomerate. I was in graduate school and well on my way to becoming the ambivalent Marxist I am today. As I tried to process it all, both from my new position as student of political economy *and* from my older one as someone who had worked within the pinnacle of the fraud, I took recourse to what psychoanalysts call a compromise formation. A way to manage in fantasy aspects of life that remain disparate, such formations reveal just how many antagonistic players one's psyche includes. Perhaps a long-dead parent returns to guide one through childbirth, or a beloved friend suddenly appears as a traitorous foe. To try to make sense where perhaps none was to be made, I imagined reading *Capital*, volume 1, with Guy and Cindy as the bubble finally popped. Maybe in that twenty-fourth-floor conference room—the site of so many General Meetings. The scene was one in which Cindy selected passages from Marx to share at the Arthur Andersen Management Training Center in Tampa, Florida, the place where she had acquired the Play-Doh technique. "It's crazy, but he actually had some really good ideas," I could hear her explain, while Guy looked on, abstemious as ever. That fantasy was still some years off, of course. As I assumed my fake Media Directorship, corporate players still had a robust stock market, an unsullied Arthur Andersen, an erect World Trade Center, and six months to go before Y2K arrived.

The reality of our end times in June 1999 meant that as Media Director, I would now be supplying Cindy with a Media Team bullet point for the weekly General Meeting's status report's "Ongoing Tasks" section. "Continues to Send Y2K Questionnaires to Key Media Vendors." For months, it had been Jennifer who had sent our team's update. No longer. I drafted my first managerial communiqué, narrating my first week as a Media Director and explaining Rick's ongoing efforts; I suggested that summer might throw a few millennial media curveballs, and if it did, the Media Team would be prepared. And I did feel oddly proud to send my prose, the fruits of my knowledge work, off to Cindy for inclusion in the status report. Then two days later, there it was, edited and amended by Cindy and appearing under the Media Team bullet point: "Continues to Send Y2K Questionnaires to Key Media Vendors."

Phase III: Contingency Planning

Continental Comportment

Readers know that the direst of Y2K prognostications did not materialize. When the clock struck 12:00 a.m., nary an automatic coffee maker-alarm clock combo went on the millennial fritz. Meanwhile, drawbridges continued to rise, airplanes remained aloft, the US dollar circulated as legal tender, and those without hard currency found that credit cards, too, functioned in those weary first moments of the third millennium much as they had in 1999. I spent the first morning of that new year having an overpriced brunch with my girlfriend in the Carroll Gardens neighborhood of Brooklyn. We drove over from Park Slope, and when I tried to pay the parking meter, I found it inoperative. My god, I thought, it's here, Y2K has arrived. Actually, January 1 is a federal holiday, so parking was free.

In terms of advertising, January 1, 2000, passed as a day like any other. Newspapers, television, radio, and new media all carried both folksy and cutting-edge reminders to purchase commodities and services and to think fondly about the enterprises responsible for already-purchased commodities and services. Did history advance so seamlessly because of the efforts of offices like mine, or was such a neat succession independent of those of us who devoted our professional selves to Y2K preparedness? What else might have happened? That realm of contingency is where philosophers often tread and so, it turns out, do Media Directors. Even as we had followed The Process and documented the existence of hundreds of thousands of clock-containing items in the Conglomerate's possession, visited the offices housing those items and documented those visits, sent thousands of Y2K preparedness questionnaires to the Conglomerate's crucial media vendors and received almost as many responses from them that no response could be offered (for legal reasons), the continued understanding around the office was that the Y2K situation remained tenuous and was perhaps deteriorating. "Predictions are getting worse," Justin announced at a midsummer Wednesday General Meeting, confusing, as often happened in office parole, subject and direct object. He then relayed that the Conglomerate's CEO, a visionary corporate consolidator and Connecticut-based sailing enthusiast, had decided to purchase a Y2K insurance policy. "I was surprised by that," our Managing Director explained, genuinely, in one of those moments where an unexpected experience of sincerity reveals just how much insincerity one had unknowingly been immersed in. Our office had been made to understand that *we* were the Conglomerate's Y2K insurance policy—and Justin the underwriter of that policy. Now that motivational buttress had been compromised.

The unanticipated insurance buy was only one of many chance moments of which Phase III: Contingency Planning was composed. As the office began to consider hypotheticals, team members had to confront the question we had so often posed: What would you do *if*... ? One had to both invoke the most disruptive of time bomb 2000 scenarios and acknowledge that, quite frankly, were any of them to transpire, advertising would be of little concern. A kind of unstated collective agreement seemed to emerge that stipulated that world-historical catastrophes—famine or war, for example—were better not discussed outright; rather, they should be hinted at, and then only subtly. Our vision of world-ending and the resources required to meet it appeared a modest one, more Norman Rockwell than Albrecht Dürer. The Conglomerate would likely not be visited by the four horsemen of the apocalypse, skeletal and haunting, lunging at history's abyss; rather, preparing a family dinner, one kitchen appliance would not work, Dad would consult the Contingency Plan, and then he would tell Mom to locate a different appliance with similar function that, somehow, was still operating.

Such discrete details of contingency planning came to me secondhand. As Media Director, I no longer attended Tuesday's all-female Analysts' Meetings. Yet even with my joke of a promotion to the managerial level or something resembling it, I was not included in Monday's all-male Managers' Meeting. I had not been present, for example, to receive the news from on high—unnamed lawyers, elite functionaries, Guy—that a fresh round of global site visits needed to be undertaken. Specialized site visits of the highest order, these meetings would focus on the millennial unknowns of media vendors and suggest contingency plans that might remediate a potential Y2K meltdown. They would bring to the same table the Conglomerate's agencies' various Media Directors and the Y2K office's Media Director (incredibly enough, me) to exchange media-specific information about the spread of eventualities.

No sooner had I learned of my revised corporate to-do list, then I was conveyed to Athens, Greece, where I found myself in a luxury hotel that abutted the Acropolis. From my suite's flower-accented balcony, there it stood, lapidary and splendidly visible on a rocky outcrop—a plinth for the sculpture of Western thought itself. When I had been told Greece would be the first stop on my months-long six-continent itinerary of "Media Contingency Plan Meetings," I was admittedly baffled, as were several team members. "Can someone please figure out once and for fucking all whether Greece is in Europe?" Justin had demanded. He meant conceptually.

Because despite weekly touchdowns in Europe, team members had yet to visit Athens on their various global tours of the Conglomerate's shops, and that omission had begun to seem problematic. One could well imagine Greece as the Belgium in our own Y2K Maginot Line. A miniscule, seemingly unimportant slice of territory would be the opening through which a proverbial invading army would march. And when it did, the outcry would be immediate. "What? You neglected Greece? What kind of slipshod outfit were you folks running?" The clock was ticking—wasn't it always?—and I can attest from experience that it's possible to travel from Midtown Manhattan to Athens' Hotel Grande Bretagne in just under thirteen hours if one makes use of the special amendments offered to business travelers: the expectant town cars and expeditious passport lines, the early boarding and even earlier deplaning.

My Athenian presence seemed both an intimate reference to my past and a sally into a corporate future that suddenly felt a lot less dismal. Not a year previous, I had been a philosopher myself, and the Ancients one of my areas of study. *The Republic*, the *Nicomachean Ethics*, the *Apology*, I'd plumbed them all, and look where they had led me. Now I was a fake Media Director, a counterfeit alumnus of the school of management consulting, a convenor of mission-critical dialogues on a global scale. If one guiding fantasy of a liberal arts education is that its truths may be translated from one conceptual realm to another, that its abstractions can be concretized and put to work, then I was that fantasy's realization as well its beneficiary. Of course one recalls the cheap thrills of corporate critical thinking: "What Socrates Can Teach You About Expanding Your Customer Base"; "How Aristotle Can Help You Rebalance Your Portfolio"; "What Plato Would Do If He Were Bumped Off His Flight." Indeed, several of the Andersen people had recently read and staged scenes from Shakespeare's *Macbeth* as part of an elective tutorial on how to develop better communication skills with clients.

I, too, relied on the Ancients to guide me through my corporate labyrinth. I almost wonder whether I did so too much, because even before I had reason to visit his hallowed ground, that forefather of philosophy, Plato, had made an appearance in my Bildungsroman. On the few occasions that Justin had needed to speak with me, for example to inform me of the necessity of these media-specific site visits, he directed me to meet him via the all-office intercom. "Leigh Claire to Justin's office in five minutes." Such announcements, rare as they were, startled me. They were emitted without warning from every team member's phone and from a series of wall-mounted speakers, including one in the women's restroom that produced an off-pitch echo. The passage of those minutes felt like a *longue durée*. Justin had the corner office, befitting a Managing Director, yet he had that room's signature mark, an expansive set of windows on two walls, hidden behind curtains drawn. He likewise kept the lights off, guaranteeing he worked in a permanent state of duskiness.

Fake Work

The first time I had been summoned—to be told of my Dallas embarkation—I approached with a sense of trepidation; I had to steel myself to enter. My Bildungsroman instructs that

```
from the doorway, I can't see
Justin himself, as a bookcase
dedicated to Yankees' World Series
memorabilia blocks my line of
vision. But the wall directly
behind his desk is animated with
a series of loose, foggy images,
reflections from his computer
monitor that appear, morph, and
disappear in sequence. I stand idly
in the doorframe, watching them
process before realizing he is
playing a video game.
```

I had been taken aback at the posture of the Managing Director, if also somewhat relieved. In those early months of corporate work, it was hard not to worry that I might (reasonably) be revealed as a fraud and summarily fired. That organizing fear had been heightened by the public nature of his summons. Indeed, it had only been the mounting evidence of fakes, oddities, and sundry misdeeds that eluded easy classification, the fact that the Managing Director spent some of his working days playing video games, for example, that over the course of some months had gradually subdued my termination anxieties.

But that exit fantasy quelled, a different concern arose. It was a query provoked by that initial visit and one that became even more structuring. Indeed, not a day passed when I didn't wonder whether I was employed by an actual global advertising conglomerate or a simulacrum of one, whether I worked alongside Arthur Andersen consultants or a pale imitation of them. Certain things seemed real enough. The building. The furniture. Team members, too, were possessed of a stubborn materiality. It was the more metaphysical dimensions that were lacking. If the Conglomerate were indicative of global capitalism, then what precisely was global capitalism? To make sense of the scene I'd found in Justin's office and all the rest of it, I recruited Plato into my text:

```
This setting. The dimness and
shadows, the confinement. It's so
reminiscent of Plato's famous
cave allegory about freedom and
enlightenment. The idea that we're
all basically prisoners trapped
in a cave with shackles, fettered
necks and fetal cognizance,
watching shadows on the cave's wall
thinking such shadows the end-
all and be-all of human existence.
Until one prisoner is freed and
ascends the cave and discovers not
only that shadows are not nearly
as substantial as the objects from
which they derive but that the sun
illuminates everything and is the
metaphorical bearer of all human
```

> knowledge. Except that I'm walking *into the cave*, the exact opposite of Plato's free soul, the receiver of truth, who leaves the cave.

(Italics in my original Bildungsroman, where their presence is understandable but obfuscating.) My hope was that Plato would guide me from darkness to sunlight, from ignorance to revelation. Indeed, these very metaphors for awakening derive from his master trope of deciphering the constitution of reality. That's maybe the only thing I had learned in college. But Plato's allegory of the cave wasn't the right structure for which to investigate corporate truths.

As though the problem were to discern whether I existed as an autonomous agent, a citizen, or an ancient slave. As though it mattered whether I could predict if the world would end on 1/1/2000 or if it would continue. Whether anyone could. No, the problem was that I was dialoging with Plato when I should have been discoursing with Marx. Or at least with Marxists. Instead, what emerged into my premillennial, pre-Marx Bildungsroman was the language of the fake, the fraud, the flimsy; a screen of corporate shadows, one could flip the light switch and illumination would prevail. If only it were that facile.

Finally, we arrive at the crux between past and present, between that initial iteration of my very first and, as of yet, unpublished book, "Bildungsroman: A Year in My Life" and this one, *Fake Work: How I Began to Suspect That Capitalism Is a Joke*, and at those interstices we find the paradox that holds these two texts together. So much of my corporate life really was fake—the Y2K bug, the Arthur Andersen consultancy, my Media Directorship, even the sweet taste found in each Diet Pepsi—and such ontologies just could not have mattered less.

The fakeness of my Fortune 500 tenure added texture and flair but not really categorical significance. Like frosting on a cake or a boutonniere pinned to formal garb—the basic infrastructure doesn't change with the decoration, however thoughtful or distinctive. Think of those anxious hours spent scrubbing canned goods and disinfecting mail in the early days of the COVID-19 pandemic: work takes its toll whether necessary or not, whether "real" or not. So much of it was useless, unnecessary, outrageous, destructive, even. So what?—none of that rendered it any less necessary for pushing the whole juggernaut forward to see another day and to have a chance to make another buck. That's what I would ultimately need to reconstruct in the philosophically mature iteration of my text (*this one*), where what's always been needed is an understanding of capitalism's ability to make money off anything, so long as someone's working and the fact that once, in 1999, that someone was me and the anything was Y2K.

Y2K, then, was part of the financial bubble and the extended joke that capitalism plays on all of us—the final silhouetted shape that dotted our own little Midtown Potemkin village. A thousand-year-old mystical anxiety plucked out of occult history to reappear as litigious, technical and able to be managed by the smartest guys in the room, Guy, Cindy, Jennifer, et al., for a price, of course. A thousand years previous, as 999 CE advanced toward 1000 CE, as historical anxieties mounted, one might have paid to smooth one's course of millennial transition, but the money would have gone to the Church with the hope of being amerced. In 1999, anxieties would mount and money would be spent, but the management consultants, not the keepers of the Holy Trinity, would claim the profits. That impending millennial event, the specter of a possible total unraveling and the concomitant need to examine our shared social organization and theological assumptions, might have provided an occasion to ask some of any democratic society's most crucial questions—What is our future? What is the nature of collective history? What shall we maintain? What shall we change? Of course, none of these questions were asked, and in their place was a single inquiry: What does The Process advise? But, still, one felt that their possibility dwelled in our shared atmosphere and that under radically different circumstances, they might have been considered.

As lingered other possibilities in Athens that did, finally, offer me its philosophical truths, mainly about the constitution of friendship and the bounds of Platonic love. My stay in Athens wasn't a solo affair. Leni was there, too. She had been assisting with several Y2K site visits in technologically unsteady Eastern Europe, and when she learned of my surprise itinerary, she decided to stop by Athens on her way back to NYC. (At a certain level of expenditure, I was to learn, corporate air travel is like interstate travel: once you're on, you can get off at different exits and just as quickly rejoin the course; after a trip commenced, team members could detour wherever they liked.) Taking advantage of the Conglomerate's "extra day" policy allotted to international travelers for purposes of time-zone adjustment, I had reunited with her in our hotel's lobby, and soon thereafter we jumped in a taxi. Our destination we gave only as "a beach," and some fifty minutes thereafter, in one of the few properly cinematic moments I experienced at the Conglomerate, we shed our clothes and leapt off a diminutive cliff into the waiting Aegean Sea. Today, I shudder to recall our own lack of contingency plans. Did we wear enough sunscreen? What if our wallets had been lifted from our clothes as we swam? Was the tide coming in or going out? Like so much of what transpired at the Conglomerate, that Greek afternoon seemed like a kind of cosmic exception, one made only because of our exceptional circumstances.

We could have been at a Midtown deli eating soggy salad-bar spanakopita, but we were in Athens. I could have been in my hotel room reviewing my materials for the next day's media-specific Y2K site visit, but I was bobbing and flipping away the afternoon in the ocean, letting the current pull me out, garnering the effort required to find my way back to shore, only to lazily repeat the experience. We could have had a businessman dinner in the vicinity of other businessmen, but we had decided on a seaside taverna, dotted with amphorae and flowers, where we proceeded to get progressively more tipsy on the heat, the wine, the sun, the feeling of bounty, the alluring strangeness of each other—Leni was my first old-world friend; I, her first queer friend. She seemed so at home in Europe, so comfortable with the idiosyncrasies of Continental life, like its strange commitment to curtainless showers and windows without screens. Flood the bathroom with every ablution! Let mosquitos breed in the resulting puddles! Europeans have other concerns, like planning their five weeks of paid holidays or enjoying a tuition-free university. We had debated the screen issue before: she was committed to aesthetic principles—windows appear more pleasing without screens; besides, she insisted, imagine their gray, likely frayed sheen on the kind of nineteenth-century twelve- and fifteen-foot windows to which she was accustomed. But the bugs, I always countered, the flies and gnats, hordes of wasps, even, in August, surely such pestilence detracts from the appreciation of a space. Neither of us would ever convince the other, and that, too, became part of enjoying our divergent pasts and the oddness of our shared present.

Always quick to quantify, team members often categorized the particulars of Y2K business travel as those that did or that didn't "count." I say that as though I hadn't, within hours of my first international site visit, adopted the practice, itself a kind of intricate private accounting. Did the time to travel to Athens and back count as labor? Did the taxi fare out to the beach and back count as a transportation expense? Did Leni's and my mutual crushes on each other count as a transgression? Or was it all subsumed under the rubric of work? One could organize one's ledger in any number of ways, just as one could recalibrate as one went along. An office attraction does make one's working day more sustainable, but only to a point. Meanwhile, the distance between the homo-narcissistic thrill of enjoying a straight crush and the tired homo-cliché of the same experience is a quickly diminishing one.

By the time we repaired, salty and sandy, tipsy no more but properly drunk, to the marble white Grande Bretagne, any number of things had become clear. The most surprising was that I had a small puncture wound in my left foot where some miniscule shard of stone had lodged itself (no one, not even Marxist critics of water, ever seems to mention how truly rocky the Mediterranean is). I'd begun worrying about the pain at dinner, before the second bottle of wine, anyway, and Leni said she could tolerate my complaining no longer. What was also clear was that

Leni thought she could attend to my wound using the rudimentary tools found in the hotel's sewing kit. And that's how I ended up supine on the bed, and Leni ended up kneeling beside me, in prime position to notice I hadn't shaved my legs, in *two days*. "Media Director!" she admonished. A corporate faux pas, yes, but in my defense, I'd be wearing pants for the site visit, and, as team members never tired of noting, I'm a natural blonde. Leni retrieved a razor and announced that in addition to her amateur surgical work on my foot, she would be shaving my legs, all in the name of Y2K preparedness. There I was, reciting lines from Platonic dialogues in my head—"But Gorgias, is not all love in some sense friendship?"—or was it the reverse, that all friendship is love?—and who knew how many sheets to the wind, more than two, anyway. The Acropolis glowed, lofty and antiquated, but passages from Plato well receded, and as I removed my pants, I was able to summon a clear thought: this may be a corporate tryst. But what alcohol giveth, it taketh away, and I sort of passed out, only to awake eight hours later to a much less seductive reality.

For as sensual as our "extra day" had been, the morning of the site visit offered a testament of the cruel downsides of embodiment. From the blinding morning light—I actually had to wear sunglasses to the hotel's sprawling breakfast buffet—to the head-wringing hangover, to the sunburn, embarrassingly more pronounced on one side of my face than the other, to the anxiety generated by a careful inspection of my aching foot. There, buried under a flap of skin but clearly visible, lay a shard of stone, one unable to be dislodged or retrieved. The physical consequences were as bad as the psychological ones. I was forced to limp in the most exaggerated, archaic fashion to avoid pain on impact. "It only hurts when you walk, right?" Leni had tried to put a positive spin on the injury over our morning espressos. But I did have to walk—into a Greek advertising agency to give my presentation. The same presentation. It was my turn to show the duck.

From that first virginal conference room moment when I had seen Cindy deliver the New Hire Presentation to the glimpse I'd caught of it after the Executive Council Meeting, some bold part of me had thought, "Hand it over, I could do that." Now, confronted with actually doing it, I was in absentia in some pretty fundamental ways: ambulation and concentration the most obvious ones, but other, less apparent deficits were in fact more worrisome: What even is a Media Director? I'd been so excited to become one it hadn't occurred to me to investigate the finer points of their existence. Some minor relief was located in the fact that a Greek advertising agency looks remarkably similar to an American one, the different alphabet excepted, of course. But there were the framed advertisements on almost every wall: the smiling subjects, some holding their inspiring commodities, other, likely basking in the services or experiences on offer—for what? I had no idea, as advertising was moving into its conceptual phase: smiling, attractive people with good skin and well-arranged teeth, their vitality and exuberance almost the point. Then Nathalie sauntered in, my Greek Media Director counterpart, with a branded demitasse in one hand and a cigarette in the other. She was kind enough not to mention that I was compromised and to seemingly overlook the awkward manner in which I grabbed at tables and chairs, railings, and anything else freestanding for support as I hobbled across the lobby. I rarely smoke, but when she offered, I leapt (not literally, which I couldn't have) at the chance for a distraction and a further stimulant.

I handed Nathalie a stapled printout of the Conglomerate's Y2K presentation. The paper version was meant as a preview of a future without technology, and together we perused the coming disaster. "On January 1, 2000, will I still have . . . ?" The duck and sledgehammer cartoon—I never did make sense of it. And our office gem: "Y2K is a documentation problem, not a technology problem." There was an addendum, too, in a sense the reason for the visit: that the Conglomerate's Media Team had contacted some of the most mission-critical Greek media vendors about their plans for avoiding millennial disaster and had heard nothing in response. I was a speedy doomsday prophet, and she an ambivalent apostle. The Dallas site visit had taken forty-five minutes, but this one was more expeditious. Soon enough, I was riding through the Athens airport on one of those elongated golf carts reserved for senior citizens and frequent fliers with medical ailments. Seated next to me was an American college student decked out in Auburn University ware with a pirate-like patch visible under the brim of his blue baseball cap and his left arm in a sling. He recognized me as a kindred spirit, apparently, after having suffered a mild concussion when the swerving mizzen sprit of a sailboat had hit him in the head. When he inquired as to my difficulties, I was more laconic; "Puncture wound," I uttered, and gestured downward.

Frequent Fliers

In New York City, things can be spectacular, or they can just go spectacularly wrong. While that sounds like a line from a Carrie Bradshaw voiceover at the beginning of a *Sex and the City* episode, it's actually what one of my college roommates advised me before I first lived there, the summer between my junior and senior years of college. An unpaid internship at the ACLU, which would later win me a vague expression of political solidarity from a would-be Managing Director, beckoned. It was to be my first adult homestead. But things seemed to be going spectacularly wrong. My girlfriend and I had planned to live together, but we broke up. I then became part of an odd grouping of three single semi-queer unemployed twenty-one-year-olds chasing down summer sublets from the back pages of the *Village Voice*. We were hours away from signing a temporary lease on a not very well converted basement dwelling, previously a pediatric dentist's office. Outlines of X-ray lamps were still visible on one wall, and a stale smell of strawberry fluoride lingered in the living room, if you could call it that—it had no windows and when the subway passed under it, the floor vibrated.

But then it happened, our own little New York story, from spectacularly wrong to spectacular. By misrepresenting our pasts, and futures, forging our parents' signatures, and moving in two friends to cover the insane rent (we had to lie about the extra roommates, too), we somehow landed a two-story East Village penthouse. About the only truthful statement on our sublet application was that one of us, me, had experience changing cat litter boxes and could be trusted to mind two solicitous Persians and a geriatric Siamese. Somehow it all worked. The five of us rotated between three bedrooms and organized a reliable front-door key-handoff system. We hosted drunken dinners on our twelve-foot pink dining table and held a Fourth of July party on our rooftop terrace.

Before moving to NYC for real after I graduated from college, I had imagined my adult life, my professional life, my I-will-have-a-career phase of being would transpire in identical fashion. That it would be similarly spectacular. But ten months into my corporate life, it wasn't. And then it was. Because no sooner had I returned from Athens than less philosophical continental cities beckoned: Madrid, Amsterdam, and Milan. And once word of a global set of media site visits had spread about the office, various team members began lobbying Justin for their inclusion in them. A manager here, an analyst there, an Andersen person to ensure compliance with The Process. In dreamy Milan, we had a swollen site-visit team of two managers, an analyst, and me. My memory has it that San Pellegrino ran from the hotel taps, that I bathed in it, even. That can't be true. But the food, the wine, the hotel's boundless marble and vines that grew up its façade and trailed into its windows, it doesn't take long before corporate travel envelopes its subjects with its feeling of childish allowance, and team members became sybarites whether or not they had visited Greece.

"This is your chance, LC," Cindy informed me at the commencement of my Y2K grand tour. She had mysteriously taken to calling me by my initials, composed of the same number of syllables as my name, in an attempt, she said, to save time. My ambitious itinerary included the opportunity to visit cities I had long fantasized about, like Tokyo, Hong Kong, and urban constellations along the east coast of Australia. There would be time for surreptitious tourism, too. There was the café in Buenos Aires where Marcel Duchamp played chess, the Zócalo and its murals in Mexico City, Pablo Neruda's house turned museum in Viña del Mar, Chile. Then there were places about which it never occurred to me to desire but were no less enrapturing once I had made their acquaintance, such as sprawling São Paulo, pine-scented Helsinki, antipodean Auckland. None of this is what Cindy meant, however. "Darren L. earned so many [frequent-flier] miles, he took his whole family to Sydney business class," she explained. "They got a club-level suite at the harbor Hyatt," she continued. Other team members had redeemed miles for Hawaii junkets; converted them into points for cruise bookings, vouchers for rental car upgrades, discounts on duty-free alcohol and tobacco purchases. I'd been in the midst of an underground economy whose currency traded in rewards and whose transactions were only now becoming apparent to me.

The Conglomerate's travel policies provided a tiered system of class allotment. Flights up to six hours necessitated coach class; flights of six to twelve hours offered business class; flights longer than twelve hours amounted to a prized first-class ticket. Suddenly, the number of mission-critical Y2K situations team members repeatedly needed to attend to throughout the Asia-Pacific region made sense (first-class tickets generate triple frequent-flier miles). So, too, did team members' preoccupation with South Africa, a fourteen-hour flight from NYC, and not just Johannesburg, Durban and Cape Town, too, had become improbable locations of Y2K concern. Meanwhile, Canada, our proximal neighbor and English-speaking sibling, home to multiple Conglomerate shops but not to any long-haul flights, was judged to be fairly Y2K-prepared. When my own flight touched down in gloomy, gray, concrete Toronto in early November, only some seven weeks before it all may have been for naught, I was one of the first Conglomerate Y2K representatives to visit, and I only did so because American Airlines was offering bonus miles to make the trip.

It would be incorrect, however, to claim that team members traveled exclusively to accumulate frequent-flier miles. Rather, they traveled for the hotels, the restaurants, to get away from their families, to find themselves in time zones so far removed from Conglomerate headquarters that who knew what team members were doing with their days and nights? Who even knew if it was day or night? The Y2K site visits to Conglomerate shops, ostensibly the raison d'être for our globe-trotting circus, rarely took more than half an hour. If they did take longer, it was because we adjourned for lunch, drinks, or dinner. Sometimes we'd begin with the first and work our way to the third. In Buenos Aires, under the counsel of several Argentine Media Directors, Leni and I consumed so much red wine at lunch that we missed our flight to Brazil—"So you'll go tomorrow," one of our Argentine colleagues casually commented. "What's the hurry?" Even a cursory recall of my presentation might have reminded him that we did have a rather nonnegotiable deadline, not that I mentioned that. Several corporate affairs were consummated under precisely such conditions, others foiled or narrowly avoided (mine, for instance). But like the United States military under Bill Clinton's second administration, during which we were in fact living, the office had casually adopted a Don't Ask, Don't Tell policy regarding sexual activity and orientation. That suited me as well as the other homosexual team member, the always well-dressed and the only thin male manager, Tim, well enough. At least, I presume; in keeping with the de facto rule, we never discussed it, including over an unexpectedly politics-oriented business dinner the two of us shared in Finland.

Team members usually sought out one of the more astronomically priced restaurants in the business district. Of course, they liked the feeling of distinction, the thrill of having the hotel concierge secure a prized booking. But it must be said that accruing credit card points from an insane dining bill was a motivating factor, too, and team members lunged for the check as though it, and not the meal, were the chief object of appetitive desire. Apparently, Darren L. once picked up a $10,000 tab in Tokyo. I became as greedy a reward accumulator as the next team member, but never in the matter of restaurants, where I strived for local color. It was one aspect of my self-betterment project in which I was determined to make my apocalyptic business tour educational, a site of cultivation. I took in a Mozart opera in Budapest; I visited the Prado in Madrid and Anne Frank's hideout turned museum in Amsterdam. And in Finland, I wanted to seek out something from the far north of that wintry country, the result of a strange interest in Nordic colonialism I had developed after reading William T. Vollman's otherwise indifferent novel, *The Ice-Shirt*. When gay manager Tim asked if I'd like to have dinner—he would be joining the media site visit, for oversight and to add managerial gravitas—I suggested a Lappish place. There we sat at a cloven-hoofed table, two corporate homosexuals surrounded by motifs of berries and mushrooms, antler paraphrenia, and pine garlands. We ate smoked rye bread and drank mulled wine out of a wooden vessel.

Talk about a queer couple. In fact, he did differ from the other managers. Tim was polite and inquisitive; he generously called Lapland's cuisine "interesting," an obvious euphemism, and said were it not for me, he'd never have tried fermented reindeer milk or even heard of intra-Arctic power struggles. He feigned concern when I related what I knew of Finnish attempts to control the Sami ethnic minority. My words "persecuted minority" hung in the air, but neither of us broached the thousand-pound reindeer in our midst, both, I think, out of respect for not outing the other. The next morning, we flew to Brussels together. Ten years after the denouement of my businessman life, he and I ran into each other at a Barneys CO-OP sale on Seventeenth Street in NYC. His boyfriend in tow, and my girlfriend, too. "LC," he said; perhaps that night in Helsinki was the last time we really spoke. Tim still worked at the Conglomerate; I told him I had become a professor. "I always knew there was something different about you!" he exclaimed, as our strange non-acknowledgement continued into a new millennium.

Ours was an exaggerated case, perhaps, but team members did not really narrate to each other what, precisely, took us to all ends of the earth and why a Conglomerate Y2K employee could always be found in the American Airlines Admirals Lounge, waiting for the priority boarding to begin. Rather, the travel was understood as a necessary sacrifice; such were the demands of The Process, one team members were willing to make to continue living in a world with advertisements after the dawn of the third millennium. As with any ideology, the system works best when there exists no distance between its structure and its perception. If team members were going to fly to Singapore—the leg-cramping hours on the plane, the jetlag and humidity on arrival—then the least the Conglomerate could do would be to reimburse team members on both a psychic and a material level. Team members layered their corporate commitments with their own individual ones: two team members, lovers, in fact, tiptoed off to Zimbabwe's storied and imperial Victoria Falls during a South African site visit; my girlfriend joined me for a five-day repose at the Ritz-Carlton in Hong Kong. We took a ferry ride to the outlying islands and delighted in the anachronism of having high tea in the Ritz's Queen Victoria Salon. During site visits in certain cities, spas were visited, as were tailors in others; food was consumed at Michelin-starred restaurants, but also at Hooters, depending on team members' whims and preferences.

`The sun never sets on the Conglomerate's empire,` I wrote in my Bildungsroman, which soon became so cluttered with the sensory impressions offered by the simple difference of travel that ascertaining a point today, some twenty years after its composition, has become its own challenge. Worse even than *On the Road*, I'm afraid. Nonetheless, several site visits stand out, as do several aberrations. Of course there was Athens, which, like Dallas, had the distinction of being a first and thus deserved a mention. Certain themes do recur, however. During many of my international media site visits, I felt the reliable tug of imposter syndrome. There I was, sitting at the Chairman's Preferred Bar, reading whatever business periodicals were available and occupying myself with the free aperitifs on offer. `"Do they think I'm one of them?"` I wondered of the other Preferred Chairmen—it's the very question that indicates the syndrome. I should have known by that point that they really didn't think of others in such a fashion, a result not exactly of narcissism but of a commitment to vague similarity and assimilation, a commitment their environment mirrored and encouraged: all business lounges looked the same; most hotels did, too; most people in them looked the same, what reason was there to assume I was any different? My sexual orientation ensured that I never grappled with an off-kilter attraction to them. Instead, Sartre-like, I became ensnared in their keyhole gaze and had to contend with a feeling perhaps more uncomfortable than desire: identification. `Am I one of them?` I asked in a section of my Bildungsroman devoted to airline lounges.

This existential equivocation reached its zenith at a media site visit in Tokyo, where, in place of an expected audience of one, sometimes two, Media Director colleagues, the site-visit team of two analysts and I were led into the agency's unexpected auditorium to find that a sea of suited businessmen awaited us. Perhaps they had taken our intra-Conglomerate communications seriously: we had sent word that the world might be ending in short order and that a group of Y2K experts would be visiting their agency to advise them of next steps. Then I arrived—sometimes with other team members in tow, sometimes solo. Unusually, our Tokyo team was composed of only women, two of whom were ecstatic that the singer Ricky Martin was staying at our hotel and could be spotted poolside and shirtless during his afternoon tanning sessions, and one of whom had never heard of him. Nonetheless, once my fellow site visitors played for me "Livin' La Vida Loca," its eponymous refrain became lodged in my mind, and to this day it forms the soundtrack to my Tokyo memories.

I had always taken some comfort in knowing I was speaking to people whose fluency in English could not be guaranteed. Perhaps I imagined it was lower than it was; perhaps they were faking it to shorten the meetings. Yet that distance in communication, real or perceived, had been crucial for me as I delivered my presentation and asked a series of absurd questions: If global technology ceased 1/1/2000, how would your agency continue its advertising operations? The Tokyo shop, however, had arranged for a translator. In an English accent, she asked me to enunciate slowly so she could select her words with the kind of care and precision a world-ending situation demanded. Yet for her to benefit from the spaciousness of my corporate drawl, I had to endure its meaning with a new self-consciousness; phrase by phrase, slide by slide, there I went.

"On January 1, 2000, will you still have..." I began. Concerns were shared about the Tokyo media market: "No Japanese media vendors responded to our Y2K preparedness questionnaire." It was one of those out-of-body, disassociated experiences, so often provoked by trauma but here provoked by management consulting. As Media Director Leigh Claire held forth, paused for translation, and then continued, a depersonalized Leigh Claire wandered off the stage, collected herself, and took notes. If I'd been thus far able to negotiate corporate imposterdom at the global executive level, then surely the intimacy of my settings helped—mano a mano, one Media Director to another Media Director. Viewing myself onstage, properly suited and making millennial pronouncements, any equilibrium I had thus far maintained was disturbed to the point that, exponentially, I began to doubt my own imposter syndrome.

Because does it qualify as imposter syndrome if the subject feeling it really is an imposter? Or if the imposter subject herself represents a larger imposter entity? By any conventional understanding, I was a lousy approximation of a Media Director. Even by any nonconventional understanding, I fell short, lacking, as I did, the essentials like knowledge of the industry, a modicum of professional terminology, an age over thirty, a subscription to *Adweek*. Indeed, only through an assumption that corporate work possesses no content other than bare life itself was my presence at all appropriate. Yet that haunting and de-individuating conclusion—which any team member, including, up until that point, me, would have protested and which no expostulation could have convinced otherwise—was gradually impressing itself on me with such force that it became hard not to accept. Such a postulate was not a rule-less assignment; to be an executive bearer of corporate nothingness one had to be cisgendered and white; middle class, at least; somewhat self-possessed, enough anyway not to be outwardly self-effacing; and sincerely indifferent to the power differentials of corporate heterosexuality.

But those conditions satisfied, the most pared-down existential minimum would suffice.

I might have said one needed the ability to "walk and chew gum," but in Greece, even that remedial combo had eluded me and to no deleterious effect. One had to occupy space. But not too much. Speak with a certain confidence, but not too often. "And the *Asahi Shimbun*" a colleague said to me in a casual Tokyo moment—one of those strange question/comment hybrids. I recognized the name from our media vendor database, and I knew the company to be a large Japanese publisher. "Yes, the newspaper," I replied. But that's all I said. Listen with even attention, but whatever one heard really didn't matter. What mattered was matter itself, in human form—that point did seem nonnegotiable. And not because artificial intelligence had yet to emerge as a historical phenomenon, or because smart computing was in its infancy, or, finally, not because a robot couldn't have been drafted into our world-preserving cause; honestly *Star Wars* character R2-D2 and his own pedestrian translator, C-3PO, could have given my Y2K presentation just as well. But a robot cannot give over its own time, and in a corporate economy, "Time is everything, man is nothing; he is, at most time's carcass," my German bard insists.[1]

In my case, however, it appeared that it was woman who was nothing, because when a muffled murmur of applause greeted my presentation's conclusion, a respite was not on offer. Instead, an anxious new chapter appeared in my Media Directorship: a question-and-answer forum hosted by our loquacious translator. Many of my Japanese colleagues' responses hewed to that awkward this-is-more-a-comment-than-a-question genre and, stranger still, concerned my appearance. My fellow Media Directors noted how unusual it was to have a young woman with blonde hair in their presence, the translator, a brunette woman herself, seemed somewhat embarrassed to convey. "It's exciting for them," she editorialized, "you know, the difference." My blonde hair color, the highlights—were these a naturally occurring phenomenon, they wondered. One Media Director's hand after another went up. How old was I and what was my marital status? How long would I be in Tokyo and what were my plans? Where was I staying and what were my recreational interests?

As odd as it felt to have the focus on my person, I can't deny it was entirely without benefit. Anything to distract from Y2K. If someone had asked about servers, routers, those thick pale blue cables that snaked seemingly everywhere in the days before

Wi-Fi, anything software related, why the response rates to our questionnaire mailing in Japan were so low, what advice I had for Y2K compliance, I would have likely taken recourse to my own contingency plan, one developed just then: namely, the contingency of knowledge itself. Perhaps I had become a convert to The Process: the future could not be known until its moment arrived, and at that point it was no longer the future. The eighteenth-century philosopher David Hume made similar claims about the present and, had I been pressed, I might have made a reference to that often-overlooked Scottish skeptic.

It was this generous, if somewhat extemporaneous, interpretation of contingency that I carried home with me from my Asia-Pacific sojourn, whose conclusion was physically in Auckland, a verdant and humid town, but conceptually on Madison Avenue, in the office of the Conglomerate's CEO. In addition to documenting all their tasks, the Andersen people arranged for executive summaries of all completed tasks to be faxed to a suite of Conglomerate interlocutors, the C-suite, to be exact: CEO, CFO, CTO, COO, anyone whose title began with that respected consonant received multiple Y2K-oriented faxes daily, and it was rare not to see a team member at the fax/printing station sending out millennial communiqués. Many, if not most, of them disappeared into the corporate netherworld, but some, even if randomly, were received and read. That seemed to have been the case with the Asia-Pacific Media Contingency Plan Meetings Executive Summary—essentially a cribbing of my notes and those of the Ricky Martin–loving analysts, recombined and approved by Cindy—which found its way by fax to an executive so high up the Conglomerate's chain of command that when several team members' town-car transported themselves six blocks east to meet with him at Conglomerate headquarters, and his office was under reconstruction, it seemed both easy and comfortable for him to lead us into the momentarily unoccupied office of the Conglomerate's chief executive officer.

Could one find a location more emblematic of the power of capitalism? If someone had asked me in those whimsical early days of employment-seeking (almost a year previous, to the day) what success would look like, I might well have said, "An invitation to a meeting in the CEO's office." I see now that some part of me had been influenced by that terrible 1987 Michael J. Fox–starring film *The Secret of My Success*, in which a mailroom boy begins working in an empty executive-level suite under a fake name. He keeps a tie and blazer stashed in his mail cart and during surreptitious elevator rides and unnoticed bathroom breaks, buttons his Oxford cloth shirt, dons his tie and jacket, and presents as an executive. The company's genuine leaders each assumes someone else must have hired him, and collectively they welcome him into their meetings and parlays; so impressive is his corporate performance that even after being revealed as a role-playing chameleon of a mailroom boy, he is celebrated and offered a top-level position. In fact, my experience wasn't so far off. Except in the film, the protagonist locates new forms of corporate knowledge and uses it to improve shareholder value. And while the stock of the Conglomerate did show a steady appreciation during my employ there, I claim no such role in its upward value.

After the Athens trip and my short *discursus* on Plato, I almost hesitate to reproduce this section of my Bildungsroman, but it does seem important. The Conglomerate's CEO had his office styled in a pronounced antiquities theme. I understood the momentousness of the occasion of my presence coincident to realizing the momentousness of the decoration:

> Since it's my first and probably last time in a Fortune 500 CEO's office, I try to be especially vigilant. At eye level, in a congruous line around the room, is a series of Greek vase—like drawings, not the pornographic kind. The togaed and loinclothed subjects are going about the everyday business of antiquity: wrestling, javelin throwing, some just standing around the Acropolis chatting or pontificating. They set the tone for the office: the faux antiquated stone desk; the stressed-leather executive chair. Everything looks intentionally worn, like it just happened to be scooped up at last week's archeological dig.

Of course, I wouldn't have been in the CEO's office were one of his second-tier commanders, the CMO, or chief media officer, our host, not having his own office redecorated in what appeared a Bauhausian tradition whose signature Mies van der Rohe chairs were visible among the plastic tarps and other renovation effluvia. And I have no doubt, had we found our way into the

CFO's lair, it might have been an eighteenth-century Parisian salon, a tenth-century Zen temple, Thoreau's cabin at Walden. At this level of corporate decoration, any time period, any singular past, could be plucked out of its autochthonous setting and transmuted into a mark of personal style. It was an approach I recognized from the Hong Kong Ritz-Carlton in which one public room cited Buckingham Palace, while the next seemed out of *Blade Runner*, and the third, a recuperated Chinese teahouse.

Our host (the man, it turned out, who had ordered the round of global media site visits) was a kind of Media Director for the whole Conglomerate and had a particular interest in Tokyo. "A tricky market," he called it. This was no occasion for Darren L.–type grandstanding; rather, demurral was in order, and demure we—two male managers, Tim, the gay one I'd visited Finland with, and another one, the amorous clandestine visitor to Victoria Falls, and I—did. "Indeed," "Yes," vigorous head nods, and so forth. Noblesse oblige, almost certainly, but the CMO treated the three of us as equals, certainly to one another and, at times, to him, too. Gay Tim made monthly site visits to Asia, I assumed for the frequent-flier miles, but his last trip had been derailed by an early-in-the-season typhoon and he'd been waylaid in Brisbane, Australia, a rerouting that would have garnered him more frequent-flier miles but that meant I was the last team member to visit one of the Conglomerate's Tokyo shops.

It thus fell to me to appraise my colleagues of the state of Japanese media regarding Y2K. It was *tricky*, I confirmed, but the turnout for our media site visit suggested a high number of interested parties—I omitted that their main interest had been in me as a sexual object—as well as a receptivity to our Y2K communications. The CMO said he was glad to hear it. At this point, the other, non-gay male manager offered a statement of basic geographical fact that nonetheless reoriented the meeting. "Asia-Pacific, the whole region, they'll [sic] go first." It's true, of course, as any recollection of the placement of the strangely configured International Date Line will immediately confirm. The new millennium, and with it any Y2K catastrophes, would begin in Pacific Island nations like Tonga, Samoa, and Kiribati, and the dominos, were they to fall, would topple from there. Like the medieval bubonic plague, trouble would arrive from the east: Tokyo and Hong Kong, on to Istanbul, then Milan, London, and a few hours later, New York. The CMO acknowledged this and said he wouldn't at all be surprised if the Conglomerate's CEO demanded from our office on December 31, 1999, an update on Tonga. Apparently, the CEO had a habit of selecting, almost at random, one of his underlings to produce some bit of idiosyncratic knowledge that, after momentary consideration, he would then relegate to whatever obscure province from which it had derived. For a few weeks, this specter indeed became somewhat of a rallying cry around our office—what about Tonga?—where it metonymized the necessary failure of the cognitive mapping we had undertaken. Some place, some country, some shop would sneak through the millennial sieve—Tonga seemed as good a bet as any.

Then there was another matter. By this point in my corporate tour, my days, my meetings, my trips were mostly in the company of men. Businessmen. And many of them I had begun to find revolting. Most of them smoked, and a few of them would, for reasons I never entirely understood, have our receptionist FedEx them packs of their preferred cigarette to coincide with their arrival at whichever far-flung location they were site visiting. Not that this habit was somehow more off-putting than the larger one it supported, but it did exemplify a different kind of profligacy. They lived in airline lounges, in hotel suites, on planes, and in town cars, most of which provided acknowledgment of being and recognition of status through Rabelaisian amounts of food and alcohol. The point is that they were dying, if slowly, and before rigor mortis set in—in some of them, it already had—they had decided in some not fully conscious way to fleece the Conglomerate of everything they could; the ill-planned dawn of the third millennium offered them an opportunity to do so. All the miles, the points, the bonuses and gifts, the duty-free splurges and business lounge debaucheries, they sought Rewards and they wanted to be Rewarded. The more time with them I spent, the less interested in them I became, until I realized I had never been interested in them per se, but in their power—and seeing them interact with our Chief Media host, I realized even that they didn't have too much of.

Of course, the Conglomerate was structured by hierarchy and rank, but our Chief host's employment, and indeed his being, was maintained at a different level, one that the prefatory C of his title captured but did not fully explicate. He appeared calm yet vivacious, well tailored and well kept, manicured and perfectly shaven, handsome even. It was this to which my male managerial colleagues aspired. It was likewise this that remained for them out of reach. (True, Tim had some of these qualities, but he had his own difficulties: he was a gay smoker.) It hardly mattered that so much of knowledge work was a performance, because they could perform a most generic, team sports–oriented, white, business-class masculinity but not much else. What little room they had for otherness was mostly directed toward Carlos, our gay travel agent, whom they often called "sweetheart"—not gay Tim, who, for obvious reasons, couldn't join in the fun of disavowed homosociality—and whom they would sometimes join for Greenwich Village homo happy hours on the company dime.

When the three of us arrived at the office after our C-suite sojourn, Cindy and I had our one and only conversation about feminism, gendered divisions of labor, and the manner in which heteronormativity left an indelible imprint on our twenty-fourth floor. Cindy was ecstatic, of course—that someone from our office, that a former member of her elite QA Team, her onetime mentee, me, had walked, even for a moment, the highest halls of corporate power. I sensed a tad of non-cognized jealousy, too, an unarticulated feeling of "Why LC and not me?" Fair enough, truly. In any world of corporate equality and meritocratic respect, were a Y2K team member to be plucked out of obscurity and plopped down *Wizard of Oz*–like in the CEO's office, it should have been Cindy. Not a single team member would have disagreed, not then, not now. Her feelings were likely complicated by corporate feminism's depressing and somewhat unacknowledged belief that there's only room for a few women at the top, to the effect that female solidarity and competition seem permanently paired. Suspended between such emotional polarity—genuine excitement and just as genuine cutthroat feelings of the constriction of her professional lifeworld—Cindy proceeded the only way she knew how. Veiled and disguised, both subtle and not, any interpretation of our exchange requires corporate hermeneut's attention to metaphor and transposed meaning, which I've taken the liberty of providing.

Cindy: "Hey, LC, can I get a copy of the meeting notes?" [*Remember, you are a woman.*]

Leigh Claire: "I didn't take the notes. Ask Tim." [*A male homosexual is just as capable of notetaking as a woman is.*]

Cindy: "Tim? Really?" [*I suppose male homosexuals and women do have a certain structural resemblance, but I've never considered why I believe this or what constitutes the similarity.*]

Leigh Claire: "Yep. Tim took the notes." [*I, too, am a homosexual; I don't need to record the speech of every straight man I happen to be in the presence of.*]

Cindy: "OK—I'll ask him." [*What consenting adults do behind closed doors is their own business. But team members shouldn't flaunt their private lives at work.*]

Floods and Fires

I've never been in a military foxhole (or a mammalian one, now that we're talking about it). Women can't be drafted into armed service, and were that policy to have changed during the late 1990s, the historical period in question, I likely could and would have skirted deployment by outing myself as a homo. But had a million different contingencies transpired otherwise, and had I found myself in trench-style ground combat, I'm fairly sure I'd be the one to disprove the old saw about atheists. As a child dragged weekly to a liberal Presbyterian church, I had often been in the company of God, but to no real effect. Then, at thirteen, the question was put to me of whether I wanted to be confirmed as a member of the church and become a god-fearing parishioner in my own right. It took me longer to select my daily outfits for middle school than to decide that, no, I'd venture through a secular life alone. And when, in that possibly apocalyptic year of 1999, events did turn biblical at the Conglomerate, I did not waver. Locusts and plagues never visited, but fire and brimstone made a cameo appearance, as did a surprising storm whose biblical intonations were frankly hard to ignore.

It was sometime late in that anxious August of 1999 that a freak midnight flood struck New York City. I have it documented in that first draft of Bildungsroman and unlike, it must be said, certain other aspects of corporate life to which I now have only textual access, I remember the rhythm of that post-diluvian day quite well. A horribly damp morning, it had clearly rained at night. Small puddles dotted the paving stones of Brooklyn's sidewalks; the asphalt had that technicolor water-mixed-with-gasoline slickness about it. But, as always, in a New York summer, it was the heaviness of the air that truly impressed—and one could have swatted at it with a machete. Still, if someone had conducted a man-on-the-street interview with me that morning, somewhere between my apartment and the five blocks to the subway, if they had asked me, impromptu, "What happened?" or solicited me to share my impressions of the morning, I would not have offered an aquatic-oriented answer.

In those pre–cell phone days, a New Yorker would assess the subway platform composition for clues and imagine her commute from there. And that morning, the F Line platform was overcrowded; the train hadn't come in some while, and there was no indication it would arrive anytime soon. So I left that station and walked a few more blocks to the N / R Line, nicknamed by locals "the Never and the Rarely," to give some sense of that train's frequency. En route, I ran into a friend who said the previous night's rain had disrupted the trains. I went home; my girlfriend was still there—she hadn't heard of the weather event but was only late to leave for her day's unpaid internship at a well-funded cancer research center. We enjoyed the moment of a late start and had sex. Then, at 10:30 a.m. I left for Midtown again—and this time I made it; forty-five minutes later I arrived into a transformed corporate world.

Cindy was perched with hawklike intensity inside a kind of

bivouac she'd created between the office door and the elevator. She had a clipboard in one hand and a pen in the other. I had barely crossed the threshold when she broadcast clear across the stand of cubicles: "LC made it!" A different voice rang back, a woman's, I wasn't sure whose, "Check." Cindy had meant to affect a tone of relief at my arrival, but her excitement won out. The woman had spent more than a year preparing the office for a crisis and now we had one: a flash flood. She herself had walked to work, she said. From the Upper West Side. Not exactly an alpine trek, but, as she pointed out, wearing a blazer and other business-casual accoutrement on a humid NYC summer morning is trying enough while waiting for an air-conditioned subway to arrive: "I walked twenty blocks!" A swift and unexpected nocturnal rain had swept through the city, Cindy related. "Some team members won't make it," she said, and, without any sense of her own drama, let a pause take hold before finishing her sentence, "into the office today." We stood in silent recognition of the other before she concluded, "New Jersey commuters, especially. Oof. The PATH train—my cousin Sarah's been saying this for years."

There's a French verb I recall from my study of the post-structuralists, *événementialiser*; a rough translation would be "to be eventalized," or to indicate the transformation of an occurrence into something eventful. Whether in French or English, that process now took hold on the twenty-fourth floor. I—and most team members it seemed, save the ones with insomnia who'd been up charting the weather at 3:00 a.m.—hadn't witnessed the actual rain, nor any other part of the flood. Manhattan hadn't become a riparian zone; Brooklyn wasn't newly littoral. Rather, deductive reasoning became the order of the day, and fantasies of this hydrologic event dominated the office: felled trees splayed across railroad tracks; North Shore, Hawaiian–like waves; electric lightning more suitable to the Southwest than to the Northeast, flashing across the urban sky. Nor did the topic cease as the working week continued. In fact, a renewed sense of energy, commitment, and foreboding was palpable. Bible-like, we were facing end times, why not add a flood? The following morning's news was awash with coverage: "WATER EVERYWHERE: THE OVERVIEW; Surprise Deluge Cripples Morning Rush in New York," read the *Times* headline.[1]

"Well, we've had quite a week," Justin announced, as he convened Wednesday's General Meeting, shaking his head with both relief and disbelief. Cindy, rightly, had all kinds of plaudits and commendations tossed in her direction. The phone tree she had set up, practically out of the ether. A collection of alternate transpiration routes she'd compiled that team members could consult to solicit guidance on getting into the office in the event of a natural or, dare one say it, technology-induced disaster. A buddy-system she organized in which team members could locate a partner either alphabetically or by neighborhood. Already she had initiated the process of assembling the materials into a binder. Steely Guy, her mentor and her boss, sat in his usual silence but with an approving glow. In the way she had saved the office, while the flood itself had exposed a terrible irony: somehow the Y2K office, so busy advising others of contingency plans, hadn't developed its own—a kind of "who cuts the barber's hair?" moment.

"We all knew to expect the unexpected," Justin continued, as he both smiled and dramatically exhaled. It seemed like he might verge into contemplation and consider the idea of contingency in and of itself: Can one really plan for something truly unknown? Instead, he took a more imperative course. He often included in General Meetings a motivational saying—"Keep up the team work," "One week gone, one week closer," etc., but a flash flood occasioned more. "It's balls to the wall from here on out. We've got four months." It was as though he ran an electrical current through the office and his charge occasioned a flurry of activity, as team members sought to seize the day while it still existed to be seized. We had lived through a flash flood, and things had gone berserk in fourteen different ways: What would an actual millennial meltdown occasion? Certainly, transportation would be imperiled, but what else?

Leni and I responded by booking two weeks' worth of contingency-planning site visits in Latin America. As we traversed Conglomerate agencies in Mexico, Chile, Argentina, and Brazil, I would handle the media side of world-ending things; she would attend to the usual quotidian world-ending affairs. So as not to get tangled up in any more untoward late-night moments, her boyfriend and my girlfriend would join us halfway through the journey. We would all rendezvous in Santiago de Chile, where we would have a few meetings and then hit the road: the Andes, the Pacific, Tierra del Fuego. The number of team members coming and going, the expanse of the Conglomerate's geographic profile, the fact that our corporate travel agent, Carlos, took a percentage of every booking as his commission, meant that not only was there room to test boundaries, there was also incentive for him to help us do so. Leni and I had learned well enough, too, the manners and routines that governed corporate travel: one had to affect a dreary, long-suffering approach.

"Well, someone's got to go do this. I'll take one for the team," a team member would sigh as she headed off for a first-class week in Europe or Asia, frequent-flier points whirling in her mind, a Post-it note list of Zagat-worthy restaurants affixed to her laptop. Meanwhile, the liberties associated with site visits tended to increase in proportion to the number of site visits team members undertook.

Team members had already visited commercial São Paulo, and Buenos Aires, too, more for the romance long associated with that "Paris of South America" city than out of any Y2K necessity, it appeared. But Mexico City and Santiago remained untouched—sites of unknown and unanalyzed Y2K risk. And now, in the "balls to the wall" era, one couldn't be too careful, or too ambitious. If someone had to go, then why not us? We had dispensation to travel to any city we desired—the only requirement was that said destination had a Conglomerate shop in it. But the Conglomerate is one of the largest advertising holding companies in the world, and any city that has an airport has a Conglomerate shop.

And how impossible that I had been to Hong Kong, to Tokyo, to Melbourne, but not to Mexico City, whose slim hour timezone difference from NYC sadly didn't provide us an "extra day," thus any touring we did would have to happen quickly. The staff at the Four Seasons advised us not to walk outside in Mexico City—the same advice I had received in Johannesburg. So we booked a hotel town car to shuttle us around the *centro histórico*, a kind of carefully choreographed corporate tour of Mexico's revolutionary past. "This whole square is sinking," our driver said of the famous central plaza, the Zócalo. "Well, I don't smell anything," Leni responded as we cruised down the Avenida

Cinco de Mayo before repairing to the hotel's quaint tequila bar for dinner and a night cap.

Our first Mexican site visit transpired nonchalantly enough. The silver-haired Media Director was polite but confided in me that his agency was understaffed and overworked and that he was of the opinion that if the world of advertising did end in a few months, he, for one, should welcome it as an early retirement. "At least keep a copy of the 'On January 1, 2000, Will I Still Have . . .? Presentation,'" I responded, like a front-door evangelizer leaving gospel material with a dismissive party. We escorted ourselves out and into a waiting taxi to convey us to another agency. And here's where my recollection falters because of events soon to come that were so fundamentally disorienting and perhaps death-defying that they've left a blank spot in my memory.

I know I was impressed by Mexico City's traffic, its smog and altitude. I know this because the relevant section of my Bildungsroman focuses on themes of air and motion and not, say, architecture or political history; there's basically nothing in those pages regarding advertising or the upcoming apocalypse. Instead, I relate the truly colossal nature of the city, soon to be superseded in my mind—and still to this day—by São Paulo. The fact that transiting from the first site visit to the second, we finally were not in traffic and had indeed reached an interstate-worthy cruising speed is of a certain narrative importance:

```
We're passing through an area
both sylvan and urban. The city
undulates with hills like waves. It
seems to expand forever, only to
```

melt into a layer of dull orange
smog against the mountains. With
no warning, or turn signal, we
cut across three lanes of traffic,
wind down an overpass, and merge
onto a long straight highway. It's
encapsulated by concrete walls on
both sides, giving it a canal-like
feel. We seep into the line of
flowing traffic. I can't see the end,
my only peripheral vision is these
concrete walls. Our green and white
VW bug taxi roars and vibrates.

As boring and vehicular as my impressions read today, they do introduce the drama: Leni screaming at me "Oh fuck! LC, the car's on fire! Fire!" It was.

Grey clouds exit the dashboard
vents unevenly. Flames lap directly
on the other side of the back
windshield. I try to scream back
in response but inhale so much
smoke that instead I just cough.
I hold my arm up, to breathe into
my lapel, reach forward and begin
tampering with the door handle. Am
I really going to jump out of a
moving car? I suppose the option
seems important. Our driver is

```
engaged in his own futility: he's
sort of half out the window trying
to swat away the smoke with a
handkerchief in order to maintain
some line of vision. As he does so
the car swerves across a few lanes
toward the embankment, where it
skids against its right side before
stalling out.
```

Somehow, we escaped. The incredible thing about entitled youth? First, we laughed. A nervous laugh, yes, and perhaps one fueled by relief, but we still emitted them, in concert, while waiting for the taxi to explode. Our suits, ruined. Our second site visit, likely another casualty. The taxi, smoldering, was emitting a noxious odor. Of all the things to die for—an unnecessary Y2K site visit. It was one of the moments where the intimation of death itself provokes a different experience of life, and one notices and commits to memory idiosyncratic, seemingly random bits of experience. I remember my beige suit, the summer one I had purchased to celebrate my fake promotion to Media Director, had been transformed into the most Dickensian shade of soot-grey, except under the lapels, which seemed now a stubborn reminder of a before time.

Leni, meanwhile, was engaged in her own private dialogue. Usually a stoic, in the way that tall people often seem removed from their shorter brethren, she had become agitated. Her Trotsky-like glasses had protected her eyes from the smoke, but at the price of their translucence, so she had removed them, and now presented as a sort of towering raccoon figure. She had been surveilling the situation, analyzing it, too, and in hushed tones she shared with me her conclusion: "I don't think it's real." I assumed she meant Y2K. No Europeans seemed to care about the impending techno-doom. Nor had our Asian colleagues. Now Mexican team members, too, had acted pretty unimpressed. Likewise, many of our friends and family in the States remained indifferent. Sometimes it seemed like our office was the lone bastion of apocalyptic belief, led by Cindy and Guy.

"No, not that," she snipped. "Of course, that's not real. I mean the fire." The case she laid out was even more disturbing than that of a consultancy using a fake crisis to bilk a corporation. That we were being set up for a robbery, a kidnapping, or worse. That we were now stranded and alone. That our only link to the world we had known before was our driver, who was watching his taxi, and likely his livelihood, burn.

As we stood by the side of the highway, I was prompted to reconsider an ominous conversation we had with Justin after the flash flood but before our departure for Latin America. He had used the all-office intercom to summon Leni and me into his cave, where he thanked us for the Y2K service we were about to undertake for the Conglomerate: if Latin Americans woke up to advertisements on January 1, 2000, we likely would have played a beneficent part, he said. This conclave was perhaps the only time Justin's public hailing of me and subsequent office visit hadn't left me in an unsettled state, but perhaps it should have because its real aim was to issue us a warning: "Remember, ladies, the Conglomerate doesn't pay ransoms." But no sooner had the clarity of his position been presented then he began to backtrack. "Because what would we do if there was [sic] a hostage situation with you two? We'd have to pay." In the moment of its utterance, I hadn't given his equivocation much thought. But now I was desperate to know, which was it?

And who would deliver the news back to the twenty-fourth floor—that two team members could not be accounted for? We would miss our next site visit. But the Mexican agency's media personnel might not notice. Or they might notice and not care. Only a few Media Directors had really embraced my presence. The most effusive, a voluble New Zealander name Becky (strangely pronounced "Beeky," but with the vowel sound so elongated, I couldn't at first recognize it, a problem I encountered throughout Auckland, including with the word "Tuesday," which somehow rhymed with "Beeky,"), who had appeared at our site visit wearing a long black, clown-like tie emblazoned with the white printed letters "Y2K!" It's as though she had been waiting for us her whole life. Finally, someone who shared her millennial concerns, she said. Had I not arrived at that Auckland site visit, Becky would have sounded the alarms—and she would have been unique for doing so.

As it happened, the taxi did not explode but rather settled into a comfortably paced melt. And the driver seemed less interested in taking us hostage or, sadly, it must be said, in helping us get to our site-visit destination than in flagging down his own roadside assistance. So there we remained, as if suspended in amber, one of those strange fossil-like specimens, unable to move, available for all to look at and examine from different angles. Some passersby honked, others jeered, most ignored us. In a certain way, Leni said, we had already been taken hostage. So psychically committed she seemed to this narrative, it felt unsympathetic to disturb it. When another taxi—indeed another VW Bug, the precise kind the hotel had told us to avoid, at risk of our lives—

pulled over and invited us in, we fled. Straight to the airport business class lounge we went. Several strong aperitifs and bowls of bar snacks later, somewhat recomposed and reclothed, we used the 800 number to phone the office and alert Justin, elliptically it must be said, to the chaotic state of Y2K preparedness in Mexico. Then we flew through the night to Chile.

The End of the End

"Man is a creature who can get accustomed to anything."[1] That's a kind of sexist, somewhat nihilistic quotation I'd discovered during my sophomore year's study of Dostoevsky's novels and one that I often trotted out to myself during my time at the Conglomerate. I had gotten accustomed to days of Cindy's Quality Assurance and its spreadsheets and to an office with Jennifer and the management of her suburban estate, and now I had become accustomed to global executive business travel. I flew to Johannesburg for a half hour meeting. I watched reruns of *The Dukes of Hazzard* in São Paulo—the Portuguese dubbing was so bad I could follow the dialogue with ease. I forgot that the Southern Hemisphere had seasons opposite that of the Northern one, and I arrived in Melbourne, Australia, smack in the middle of their frosty August winter without so much as a sweater to accompany me.

As fall of 1999 pressed on, a workweek somehow always concluded in the American Airlines Admirals Lounge at London, Heathrow—the worst of the business lounges, by far, but the airline was a Conglomerate client, and we were duty bound to them by mercantile ties. There I could be found boarding one of the hourly flights back to New York. The patterns and repetitions of global travel started to feel expected and commuter-like. The

North Atlantic arc with its southern turn toward Newfoundland four and half hours into the flight, a typically nervous moment for me as shifting air currents above the ocean-to-land transition often occasioned turbulence. Same thing with crossing the equator, where global wind and ocean streams collide and contradict each other, generating pockets of unstable air, seemingly always in the vicinity of whatever flight I happened to be on.

Even under the best of flying conditions, repeated circumnavigations of the earth can engender stark visions. Sometimes, unmoored, sailing thirty-five thousand feet above who knew what Pacific atoll (maybe Tonga), I'd imagine that the apocalypse had already transpired, that whatever was under our speeding 747 was the static landscape of another era, but that the world I had departed from on my embarkation had expired and the plane would just keep flying, ghostship-like, in perpetuity. Among other things, that surreal fantasy meant that my ultimate community, those with whom I'd share whatever social contracts were still possible after the end of the world, would be the occupants of the business-class, or sometimes first-class, cabin: the Guys and Justins, the Cindys and Darren L.s, the straight managers and the closeted gay ones. Rather than banish such fantasies and let them depress my global itinerary, I embraced them and on I flew.

I began to award myself small, informal writing residencies to work on "Bildungsroman: A Year in My Life" without the interruptions of coming and going, company meals, and managing my various mileage and reward accounts. I left Friday night for a Monday afternoon site visit in Stockholm, a formal and quiet city whose atmosphere reflected my new writerly mood and whose selection of saunas offered what I needed to feel refreshed as we prepared for the final stretch. I hadn't gotten far into the writing of my earliest drafts of my Bildungsroman before I realized that I would need to read more than the *Wall Street Journal* and *Adweek* to compose a corporate tale of the magnitude I desired. My long-haul flights became study halls of sorts, for the most divergent and unlikely of bibliographies. Jill Ker Conway's *The Road from Coorain*; David Foster Wallace's insufferable essays; Dan Savage's adoption memoir I read over the Kalahari Desert en route to South Africa; *Mao II* I read in Oslo, in London, and in between. It was surely those many studious airborne hours in which I began to see that, come what may on January 1, 2000, I would need to excuse myself from a Fortune 500 future.

By December 1999, the Conglomerate's Y2K office reached the point of no return. Nothing more could really be done, a common enough cliché on the approach to any moment of finality but one particularly apt in our case since nothing really had been done. Neither could time speed up to meet our heightened expectations. Nor could it slow down to allow for the correction of newly discovered oversights. The travel diminished, too, and team members whom I'd last seen lounging under a shaded terrace in Rio or breakfasting at a buffet fit for the Queen in London were again denizens whom I passed in the office kitchenette, Pepsi product in hand. To mark the progress of the calendar and to demarcate our work, team members did what they did best, namely, preside over the expenditure of large sums of corporate cash. With most air travel suspended, team members trained their focus on accruing hotel reward points. A series of suites were booked at hotels around Midtown so that team members could monitor the developing Y2K situation across the collection of global time zones with which so many of us had become familiar. Indeed, one team member was assigned to keep tabs on Pacific Island nations. These graveyard shifts did not require remaining awake, only sleeping within a several-block radius of the office—and with whomever one pleased. Christmas and New Year's holidays were revoked, of course, but what that meant, in fact, was that team members could enjoy a series of multicourse dinners on the Conglomerate's tab, including those inflated prix fixe menus that always seem to pop up around holidays.

With limited time remaining, certainly in the office and possibly in the world, I began the process of reviewing my own documentation. The "Get to Know Y2K" binder, compiled, I could now tell, by Cindy, but for months lying dormant in the kitchenette next to a stack of unopened and unrefrigerated Parmalat milk containers, offered a compendium of analyses whose predictions ranged from maudlin to worse. One could find a scenario for every imaginable form of social breakdown: government collapse, an ensuing civil war, financial systems gone berserk.

Yet the mood around Midtown seemed the furthest thing from that of end times, unless end times are distinguished by towering Christmas stockings, holiday wreaths the size of tractor tires, and candy cane–flavored cocktails. I have vague but undocumented memories of a Midtown cigar bar in which there was parked inside some classic sports car as a decoration—maybe a 1960s Aston Martin?—and whose drinks were named after 1980s financial instruments: a poison pill, an LBO (leveraged buyout offer), a Killer Bees, a Bear Hug, and so on. Not that those dated terms of corporate chicanery concerned team members: the buoyancy of the Conglomerate's stock price matched that of the atmosphere, and team members who had taken some of their salary in options were feeling festive indeed.

Then it happened. Or didn't, depending on one's perspective. Y2K.

And like a Modernist novel whose conclusion one knows will not provide an ending, to say nothing of any éclat or grand reveal, our mission-critical moment, our finale—composed of the scaffolded segments of temporality that team members took such pleasure in delineating: second, minute, hour, day, week, month, year, decade, century, and, yes, millennium—came and went as any other had and as many other would. It seems both necessary and anticlimactic to state what everyone now knows full well. We survived and did so with minimal difficulties. Even inaugural Tonga emerged into the post-Y2K era unscathed. Cindy dutifully reported that some automatic toilets in Singapore hadn't flushed properly, stuck as they were in an expired and asynchronous world order. Other team members scoured news sources for tales of Y2K glitches and niggles and did compile a modest list, including electric garage door openers whose open and close buttons had become reversed; an odd selection of already-odd Sharper Image gadgets—think of an individual egg poacher or a solar-powered backscratcher—which had no discernable clock control but that had nonetheless broken down somewhere on the momentary midnight bridge between 12/31/1999 and 1/1/2000; an industrial blender at a Wendy's-supplying cattle-culling facility in Alberta, Canada, whose whirl wouldn't cease even when unplugged from a power source.

But by the time team members reconvened in the conference room on the bright, crisp, and bathetic morning of Monday, January 3, 2000, even the foregoing compendium of millennial malfunctions seemed little more than a set of curious examples, representatives of a larger case of something—what, exactly? Oh, right, techno-induced social collapse on a global scale—whose dimensions had already begun to recede from our Y2K office's collective consciousness. While I remain unsurprised that team members didn't engage in a public, Mao-style self-criticism session, I continue to find it slightly disconcerting that the entire event of Y2K disappeared from office discourse as though censored and that individual team members adopted an almost amnesiac approach to a time period that so many of us had let so eventfully structure our lives. There was no communal self-reflection, no "Why did we do this?" More one felt a sense of sequence. Then this happened. And then this.

It turns out that not only does corporate work possess no content other than being and time, but corporate history doesn't even possess that. I look back at my Cindy-approved site-visit notes from a smattering of mission-critical locations, some parts of which were indeed interred in paper form in a climate-controlled New Jersey document warehouse, where they would have been maintained for a certain number of legally appropriate years until said warehouse would have arranged for their obliteration, and I see nothing so much as a void:

```
*Johannesburg: "Things are difficult.
Some copper pipes and wiring were
stolen during a recent break-in.
Media Director explained most
agency personnel possess Australian
passports and might relocate. Says
Y2K can't be any worse."
```

*Melbourne: "Few people in Aus. concerned about Y2K. Media Director says they'll be OK and says she enjoys receiving visitors from NYC because we spring for such nice meals. We had Thai."

*Milan: "Media Director out sick with stomach bug. We left our presentation materials with assistant, Matteo. Agency 'on holiday' for next month."

They indeed say nothing other than that some team member had visited. An analyst had related millennial concerns, an Andersen person had suggested contingency plans that aligned with The Process, a Media Director had conveyed that the media vendors in said country had failed to respond to the Conglomerate's Y2K preparedness survey, and so on.

Once an event has passed, the event is gone, and the discourse that both documented it and was produced by it may not reflect certain truths but perhaps only need deliver the central truth of fake work: it doesn't matter what happens, only that something happens, and it doesn't matter who does it, as long as someone does it, and, for that matter, it doesn't matter to what end whichever what and whomever who are ultimately directed; Y2K was as good a forward benchmark as any, but such uniqueness offers style not substance and any event would have done.

I have a Bildungsroman's worth of examples of this corporate construct, but perhaps none have the clarity of what I always referred to privately as "Cindy's walk." After so much time, I can still sense her pattern; her slightly heeled boots padding along the worn beige carpet; her affect, always open and inquisitive; her presentation, always professional; her blazer, always unbuttoned. The Andersen people—distinct as they were—worked 8:00 a.m. to 5:00 p.m., not 9:00 a.m. to 5:00 p.m., as did Conglomerate employees like me. Every morning at 9:05 or so, once the Conglomerate people had filled out the middle mass of the office—an off-white sea of four-foot-tall Formica partitions where the receptionist and her radio sat; where my charmless cubicle had once hosted me, and then Rick; where the shy and pale IT people holed up, chatted amongst themselves, and maintained our databases—Cindy emerged from her office with Kant-like punctuality and strolled the rectangular perimeter of our skyscraper's twenty-fourth floor.

Her stated purpose was to offer morning salutations and to sympathize with team members who had endured difficult commutes and other transport tsuris, information about which she seemed uncannily already to have at her disposal. Sick passenger on the 3 Train? Signal malfunction on the F track at Thirty-Fourth Street? Traffic backed up on the lower deck of the George Washington Bridge? Delays on the southbound New Haven Line? She knew about each one. While checking in, she casually reminded those with whom she was conversing that the Andersen people had to come in an hour earlier, that they were contractually bound to do so, and that she'd already been working an hour. Hers was a route whose completion took about an hour—the same hour that she had made it her mission to expose had been consumed by the expedition itself.

It took the Conglomerate's Y2K office a little more than a year to prepare for *the year*, 2000, and during the year of preparations, that year itself disappeared, and with it, all of our preparations—save this, my Bildungsroman, whose content has honestly been so transformed in the writing of *Fake Work* that it too might well be considered part of the turnover. The main addition, of course, has been of theoretical heft, which, ironically, appears as theoretical simplicity and which I could not have composed during my actual days as a Media Director. For one thing, I was too busy managing my frequent-flier account. For another, it was only years of post-Conglomerate study that allowed me to understand in anything more than a phenomenological register the degree to which most of what I had spent my corporate time doing had been empty work, useless work, fake work. And, more importantly, the degree to which its very fakeness was beside the point. Sure, it helped matters and smoothed our course. The mind shudders to consider what having to amend millions of lines of computer code the world over to avoid a millennial meltdown would have required. But the fact of its fakeness remains less interesting than the fact of its generalizability.

As for me, I couldn't have thought *Fake Work* without reading Marx, but I couldn't have appreciated Marx without my employment alongside Andersen and at the Conglomerate. Somehow, together, the synthesis of text and job provided me exposure to the outrageous sense of contradiction that his subject—what it means to labor in a capitalist economy (which has since become my subject)—demands. This truth I really do owe to my former team members. In a scene rife with sticky oppositions, Cindy, Guy, Justin, Jennifer, et al., my corporate chorus of sorts, loyally arrived onstage in crucial moments to instruct me in the ways of their working world, where everything was both exactly and exactly not what it seemed. The full emptiness of the office; team members occupied with absolutely nothing; the nonexistent emergency that daily motivated all of us; those deemed society's best and brightest doing its most unimportant work; resources marshaled as though they had an expiration date. In a way, they did. But it certainly wasn't December 31, 1999. It was more like always.

And that's the other lesson. If fake work takes time, real capitalism takes money, and some entity's got to spend it. Why not the Conglomerate, a true multinational concern with a hoard of cash just looking for a place to call home? Stocks can be bought back and dividends paid, some liquidity preserved and bonuses offered, but a market requires transactions in both this and that. This, goods, like the real estate where the Conglomerate rented a skyscraper floor for our Y2K office, the plane tickets and computers, the office supplies and hotel rooms. And That, services: the Andersen people, foremost. Guy, Cindy, Jennifer, and Darren L. each billed for every photocopy made and binder created, for every meeting attended and amusement park visited. Less-imposing human trades were procured, too: the Conglomerate's own employees, like me, the cleaners, the drivers, and the travel agents; the temp-staffing agencies and the food delivery people who dutifully arrived each morning with still-warm English muffins and watered-down coffees from the same delis to which Leni and I would daily retreat for lunch.

Money leaves a business only to return to it. Circulation and circle share a lexical parent. That pairing, too, was a conceptual easement offered me by my corporate chorus. The local scene of instruction had as its unsurprising setting team members clamoring for more air travel rewards, specifically on the New York City-to-Los Angeles route. Recall the basic Conglomerate rules of engagement that state that flights six hours and above offer business class allowance; under six hours, coach. Recall, too, that business class offers twice the frequent-flier mileage. And now the quandary, at once philosophical and practical. NYC to LA clocks an exactly six-hour flight time, give or take those fickle head winds, and only five and half hours return, a speedup traceable to an easterly tail wind boost. Even the most seemingly factual codes of corporate governance require some interpretative nuance, and General Justin would have to render a judgment: In what carriage class would team members traverse the continent?

After initially issuing a decision that no one, no doubt including him, desired—team members will fly economy to LA—he amended his ruling and declared business class for all when flying over fly-over country. His reconsideration was the talk of the kitchenette for a few brief hours one meeting-less Tuesday morning, and multiple Pepsi-retrieving team members weighed in. What magnanimity, I thought. Others did, too. But not so Jennifer, for whom all human behavior had a transactional element, if not an overriding character. I intercepted her expounding on the LA Question mid-conversation, with heretofore unmentioned Andersen person, the Ichabod Crane–ish Chad, who—it still seems impossible—addressed his female colleagues, including Jennifer, Cindy, and me, as "girls." "But you know what, at the end of the day . . . ," Jennifer began.

It was one of her oft-chosen clichés of historical progress, second only to "going forward." Use of the "end of the day" phrase catapulted its speaker ahead of time, and ahead of any interlocutors, to some hypothetical sunset where, with sober senses and passions dispelled, said speaker could retrospect and pronounce truths not yet available to others. The phrase so often introduces the speaker's individual viewpoint dressed in a veneer of universalism and inevitability. It probably did here, too, but Jennifer's interpretation, while uncharitable, was just as likely unchallengeable. "At the end of the day," Jennifer insisted, "the Conglomerate has the American [Airlines] account." Whatever money the Conglomerate shelled out for business class fares would redound to it in the form of advertising contracts from American; same with hotel chains, rental car conceits, and consultancies, too. The Conglomerate had engaged a consultancy, Arthur Andersen, to erect an anti-Y2K lawsuit barrier; Andersen would engage the Conglomerate to advertise its services to potential clients the world over. Marx, by the way, ultimately declares capital a spiral, not a circle—in a true circle there would be no growth, no outward expansion. But, then again, Marx never worked with management consultants.

Afterward

Weeks and Decades

The first thing that must be said is that, yes, an afterward existed. And still does. Bolshevik leader and Marxist theorist Vladimir Lenin, in the thick of twentieth-century revolutionary turmoil, once proffered that "there are decades when nothing happens and then there are weeks when decades happen."* The final seven days of the second millennium did not compose one of those history-churning weeks. Rather, they were assimilated into one of those decades when "nothing happens," the 1990s. That's not quite fair, obviously. The band Nirvana emerged and with it an entire grunge scene that included the vaunting of plaid flannel shirts to a position of haute couture. An American president was impeached for receiving an extracurricular blow job from an unpaid intern. I went to college. I graduated. I got hired at the Conglomerate. Meanwhile, the state form that Lenin bequeathed, the Union of Soviet Socialist Republics, ceased its being, and when it did, something of a unanimous

---

* The quotation is widely attributed to Lenin but that is just as widely understood as apocryphal.

vision of an economic future emerged: capitalism or bust, baby. Tepidly by 2001, and certainly by 2008, the sentiment had been somewhat revised, and a different conjunction included: capitalism and bust.

Team members wasted no time in becoming accustomed to saying "the aughts" and in adjusting themselves to new professional futures. The Andersen people would be rolling off the Conglomerate's Y2K project and rolling on to new projects with other clients, for a year anyway, until their firm disintegrated. The Conglomerate's male managers had mostly come from individual Conglomerate shops, and they would mostly be returning to those shops. Poor Rick and other temps would be sent back to Americareer for temporary placement in other firms, a rotation that could last ad infinitum as long as their hours never approached full-time, thus mandating employer-covered health insurance. Those of us who had been hired in an exclusive Y2K-capacity, Leni and me, among other female analysts, would be absorbed and dispersed into the Conglomerate if we so wished. I had been offered the role of an assistant to a junior account manager at one of the Conglomerate's public relations firms in Tribeca. Location-wise, it far surpassed my Midtown perch. The office had cutting-edge angular furniture, some of it a copyrighted shade of purple; a kitchenette with more than Pepsi products; and the framed advertisements I'd become so accustomed to seeing on office walls. It was indeed as cool as work could be. But fringe benefits like my own office, no real supervision, and carte blanche access to business class travel on a global level would be consigned to the second millennium. Still, several team members told me I could prosper there were I to really commit to a life of corporate publicity.

The last executive decision I made as Y2K Media Director was not to steal the Conglomerate laptop to which I had become so attached. It contained many of the archival aspects of the Conglomerate's Y2K project, including itineraries, agendas, status reports, questionnaires, responses, nonresponses, a copy of the inventory database, and, of course, my Bildungsroman, in its first, original form. Sure, my expense reports had been padded and trips, whole continents really, had been visited under less than mission-critical circumstances, and yet, absconding with a piece of office equipment seemed one petty robbery too many. So I copied its contents on to a boxy little grey Zip disk, which promised a kind of documentary permanence but whose technological infrastructure actually became obsolete after a few years. In keeping with office ethos, I had everything in paper, too, but that computer had become something of an amanuensis to me, and it felt momentous to sever the link. The experience did end up being a limb-like loss because, for some time after I left the Conglomerate, I had the ghoulish feeling that some part of my life there had been cut off but not fully amputated.

Associations to the Conglomerate seemed omnipresent. They were omnipresent. The Conglomerate produces about half the world's advertising. Pop-up ads on websites, themselves a nascent form of advertising in 2000 and one the Conglomerate pioneered, reminded me of my corporate past; so did subway posters, highway billboards, glossy spreads in the *Sunday Times Magazine*, and the annual hoopla around television commercials on Super Bowl Sunday. Once I'd integrated back into civilian life, my Admiral status lapsed, my hotel points dwindled into single digits (not that I was staying in hotels anymore), black town cars with tinted windows, now just more traffic I'd pass on my walk to the subway, I realized that I would need a patron to continue working on my Bildungsroman with any degree of dedication. When that plan fizzled, I interviewed for a PhD program, where my soon-to-be doctoral supervisor, one of the vanquished Sokal hoax poststructuralist academics, of all people, was himself finishing an ethnography of corporate knowledge work and—wouldn't you know it—the firm at which he had undertaken his field work was owned by the Conglomerate. I explained to him that the thesis I intended to pursue as my dissertation would not be set in a specific shop, but rather on the Conglomerate's global level.

That project never happened. Or rather, it's happening now, in dramatically different form and several decades late. In the course of returning to my Bildungsroman and resuscitating it into the more manageable genre of a Marxist-inflected, queer, auto-theoretical work memoir—if that's what it has become—I tracked down several of my former team members to see what they had made of their third-millennial lives. They really did have names like Tom Smith, Dave White, Amy Peterson, and so on, and many of their titles were Lead Analyst, Senior Consultant, Strategy Ops, all of which have colluded to make it difficult to locate a specific individual with forensic certainty. Guy, for example, has all but vanished. Like an aircraft lost in the Bermuda triangle, his total digital absence defies explanation.

I did find Cindy, unconsenting bearer of so much of my twenty-three-year-old writerly attention. She has a new consultancy position and a defunct Twitter account, one whose usage looks to have been retired several years ago under apparently benign circumstances. Sometime in 2014, however, she took a business trip overseas. She tweeted a photo of herself in cramped airline quarters. Her dinner tray looked discouraging enough and she had been forced to balance it awkwardly on her left pantsuited knee; so unintuitive the spatial configuration of the cabin and unergonomic the seating that the pathos her post intended was easily generated, in this recipient at least. But I wasn't her audience. She had tagged the offending airline and turned her tweet into a missive: "Hey [@Airline]," she repined, "your business class sucks!" Could it really have been the same person with whom, even after so many years, I continue to associate business decorum, corporate savoir faire, and managerial pleasure?

Jennifer, my once officemate and Media Team antagonist, as noted, turned herself into her own corporate archive, a for-profit entity, and thus allowed me to synthesize aspects of her life's journey with mine.

I identified Justin, too. Still alive and evidently thriving, he recently appeared on a podcast for Yankees fans evocatively titled "Where Are Your Balls?" (Not exactly that, of course, but its title did mingle sporting and testicle references.) Different baseball enthusiasts visit the podcast in guest capacity, I gather, to share lifestyle tips with their fandom community. Justin dispensed advice on iPhone security and offered suggestions for weeding spam out of one's inbox: "Ask yourself this before you click on a link that offers free-whatever waffle cones," he queried his listeners—his voice's disembodied presence immediately transporting me back to those all-office intercom announcements—"Can you really get something for nothing?" He had indeed become some kind of technology executive at the Conglomerate. I suppose I misjudged him, too. As Cindy seemed a paragon of corporate poise, Justin appeared to me as the opposite, already dead in some truly material way.

Leni required no historical investigation. She and I remained in touch for some years after the predicted end of modern technology, but our friendship never had the intensity it did during our Conglomerate days. It's hard to reorient after an unconsummated crush and an unarrived apocalypse. She had always planned to show me Vienna among our Y2K travels, but we never made it—some part of her no doubt deeply ambivalent about any such Austrian homecoming. When I did visit that ornate city, finally, alone, after so many years, for an academic conference, I was surprised by its myriad and colorful alleyways, how their cobblestone paths would wind and narrow, then suddenly open onto the grandest bourgeois *platz*. With no intention of doing so, late in a Viennese afternoon, I found myself standing under Mozart's slightly off-kilter eighteenth-century wood-framed second-story dwelling. Of course, I imagined Leni's journey from that Old World to Midtown. It always had seemed a counterintuitive move to me, but she embraced it. In the third millennium, she remained in New York and became a paralegal.

And what did I become? A Marxist? An English professor? A writer? A parent? Middle-aged? I suppose, yes, a little of each. I left the Conglomerate wanting to write but without much support to do so, so I became a professor, one whose interest in corporate economics morphed into a twenty-year study of political economy and its relationship to contemporary culture. I did author three books in that vein; two of which, I think, are good, or good enough anyway. It was their publication and moderate success that enabled me to say, to myself most of all, really, that the time had come to tell my first economic story and to finish my first book. The one I always wanted to write.

Acknowledgments

It took a lot to return to this project and finish it (finally!), but before I thank those who saw me through to the end, I want to thank those who were there at the beginning. Foremost, Dehlia Hannah, who not only read but lived early drafts of this book. And, of course, thanks to all team members at Arthur Andersen and the Conglomerate—what a time we had.

This go-round, I've had more critics and a better idea of what to ask for and what to accept as criticism. Thank you to Phanuel Antwi, Erik Baker, Michelle Chihara, Max Haiven, John Munro, Lauren Oyler, Charles Petersen, Lily Scherlis, Cecilia Sebastian, Matt Seybold, and Hadas Weiss. Part of this book appeared in *n+1* and working with editors Lisa Borst and Tess Edmonson was a real treat. A very special thanks to John McDonald at Haymarket for helping me turn a baggy manuscript into an actual book. Thanks, too, to everyone at the Genres Against Markets workshop that Max Haiven and I organized with generous financial support from the ReImagining Value Action Lab and the Alexander von Humboldt Stiftung. I appreciate as well a PSC-CUNY Research Foundation Award for a smidgen of time away from teaching to dot last i's and cross last t's.

And to my family, Caroline, Momma, and Lion—thank you for everything.

Notes

Prologue: The Almost End of the World
1. Ross Laver, "Millennial Madness: 'A Few Years Ago, Only the Geeks Cared about the Year 2000 Computer Program,'" *Maclean's*, November 23, 1998, 99.
2. Antonio Gramsci, *Selections from the Prison Notebooks of Antonio Gramsci*, trans. and ed. Quintin Hoare and Geoffrey Nowell-Smith (London: Lawrence & Wishart, 1971), 9.

Millennial Transitions
1. Peter de Jager, "Doomsday 2000," Computerworld 27, no. 36 (September 6, 1993): 105–9.

"Il n'y a pas de hors-texte"
1. Donna Haraway, *Modest_Witness@Second_Millennium. FemaleMan_Meets_OncoMouse™* (New York: Routledge, 2018).

Write What You Know
1. Karl Marx, *Capital: A Critique of Political Economy, Volume One*, trans. Ben Fowkes (London: Penguin Books, 1992), 279.
2. Marx, *Capital*, 280.
3. Marx, *Capital*, 342.
4. Karl Marx, *The Eighteenth Brumaire of Louis Bonaparte*, ed. Saul K. Padover (New York: McGraw Hill, 1972), 245–46.

My Putative Promotion
1. Cecil Rhodes quoted in Hannah Arendt, *The Origins of Totalitarianism* (New York: Meridian Books, 1958), 121.

A Total Bitch and an Absolute Fraud
1. Bill Keller, "Enron for Dummies," *New York Times*, January 26, 2002.

2. Ianthe Jeanne Dugan, "An Andersen Old-Timer Recalls When Prestige Was Bottom Line," *Wall Street Journal*, July 15, 2002.
3. Reed Abelson and Jonathan D. Glater, "Enron's Collapse: The Auditors; Who's Keeping the Accountants Accountable?" *New York Times*, January 15, 2002; Richard W. Stevenson and Jeff Gerth, "Enron's Collapse: The Auditors; Who's Keeping the Accountants Accountable?" *New York Times*, January 20, 2002; Alex Breneson, "Enron's Collapse: The Accountants; Watching the Firms That Watch the Books," *New York Times*, December 5, 2001.
4. Mark Maurer, "Arthur Andersen's Legacy, 20 Years After Its Demise, Is Complicated," *Wall Street Journal*, August 31, 2022, www.wsj.com/articles/arthur-andersens-legacy-20-years-after-its-demise-is-complicated-11661938200.

A Tepid Marxist and a Bubble Popped

1. Karl Marx, *Capital: A Critique of Political Economy, Volume One*, trans. Ben Fowkes (London: Penguin Books, 1992), 168.
2. Peter de Jager, "Doomsday 2000," *Computerworld* 27, no. 36 (September 6, 1993): 105–9.
3. Paul M. Sweezy, Harry Magdoff, John Bellamy Foster, and Robert W. McChesney, "The New Face of Capitalism: Slow Growth, Excess Capital, and a Mountain of Debt," *Monthly Review* 53, no. 11 (April 2002).
4. Robert Brenner, *The Economics of Global Turbulence: The Advanced Capitalist Economies from Long Boom to Long Downturn, 1945–2005* (New York: Verso, 2006).
5. Karl Marx, *The Eighteenth Brumaire of Louis Bonaparte*. ed. Saul K. Padover (New York: McGraw Hill, 1972), 245.
6. Walter Benjamin, "Paris, Capital of the Nineteenth Century," in *The Arcades Project*, trans. Howard Eiland and Kevin McLaughlin (Cambridge: Harvard University Press, 2003), 88; Walter Benjamin, "Central Park," trans. Lloyd Spencer with Mark Harrington, *New German Critique* 34 (1985): 32–58.
7. Fredric Jameson, *Brecht and Method* (New York: Verso, 1998), 17.
8. "The Outlook," *Wall Street Journal*, May 4, 1998, www.wsj.com/articles/SB893991934722931500.
9. "Toward a New Internationalism," *Monthly Review* 52, no. 3 (July–August 2000).

My Joke of a Promotion

1. Jared Diamond, *Guns, Germs, and Steel: The Fates of Human Societies*

(New York: W. W. Norton, 1999), 309.
2. Karl Marx, *Capital: A Critique of Political Economy, Volume One*, trans. Ben Fowkes (London: Penguin Books, 1992), 342.

Frequent Fliers
1. Karl Marx, "The Poverty of Philosophy," in *Karl Marx and Frederick Engels, Collected Works, Volume 6, 1845–1848* (London: Lawrence and Wishart, 1976), 127.

Floods and Fires
1. See the article in its original context from August 27, 1999, section A, 1.

The End of the End
1. Fyodor Dostoevsky, *The House of the Dead, or, Prison Life in Siberia* (London: J. M. Dent; New York: E. P. Dutton, 1911), 80.